LifeShapes | *the Semi-Circle*

LIVING IN RHYTHM WITH LIFE

MIKE BREEN

Published by 3DM Publishing

Design: Blake Berg

ISBN: 978-0-9965300-7-1

3DM Publishing

3dmpublishing.com

This book is dedicated to our daughter Libby, Gavin, Finley and Penny, who have such fruitful lives already—much more on the way.

CONTENTS

INTRODUCTION

I t was the late 1970s, and I was ready to take on the world. Fresh from seminary, I was passionate to serve God. My work would have real meaning. I was going to make a difference in people's lives.

My first job was as a youth worker, and I headed for the inner city. I didn't know it at the time, but it might as well have been an unknown primitive island in the Pacific. My ministry was in a difficult inner-city neighborhood called Hackney, located in the east end of London. I was single at the time. Sally, my childhood sweetheart, was still in college in Sheffield and would join me a year later after she had graduated.

I rented an apartment in a place called the Kingsmead Estate, built in 1938 as the first planned social housing in London. The locals had given Kingsmead a new name: Devil's Island. On the day I was to move in, I went to get my keys from the housing manager. She gave me the keys, but not before she took the boards off the windows and doors. This was not the sort of welcome I was expecting.

She looked at me and asked, "Where's your stuff?"

"Well, I thought I'd move in on Friday," I replied.

The housing manager looked at me with a combination of disbelief and pity. She walked away shaking her head. I was as green as the grass, and I was going to find out very soon why she pitied me.

I came back on Friday with all my worldly belongings. Turns out I didn't need the keys after all. The door was kicked in and the apartment was empty. All of the radiators had been torn off the walls. My first lesson in inner-city living was that radiators brought a high price at the local pawnshop. People would go to empty apartments, rip radiators off the walls, and leave the water pouring out onto the floor. I wish I'd read this in the welcome literature, but I learned it the hard way.

> FOR MONTHS AND MONTHS I HAD WORKED ENDLESS HOURS TRYING TO PRODUCE WHAT I PERCEIVED TO BE A FRUITFUL MINISTRY.

My new apartment was covered in brown sludge—I'll leave that to your imagination—and had no heat. It was the middle of November, and for six months I had no hot water. I got to know my neighbors very well by asking them if I could use their bath.

So that was the beginning of my inner-city ministry for severely disadvantaged young people. But in spite of my raw introduction to Devil's Island, I arrived at work full of enthusiasm. I was ready to make a difference to the street kids of Hackney. Nothing would put out my fire!

Fortunately, I had a pastor by the name of John Pearce who took one look at me, saw past my passion and naïve zeal, and understood me completely. He had seen it before—young evangelical youth pastors who came from the suburbs to work in urban areas were almost certain to burn out. He said to me, "Now, Mike, you're like all the other young guys who come and help. We're so grateful for it and we're glad that you're here and we hope you stay a long time."

So far so good. We were on track with each other, but I had a feeling there was more.

He continued, "But you have no idea how to balance your life. So I'm taking this ten-pound note and I'm putting it in an envelope for you. I'm putting the envelope in my drawer. It's for your ticket home when you burn out."

This was not the kind of "welcome-to-the-ministry" pep talk that I was expecting! What was this man on?

"John, what do you mean?" I asked incredulously.

He said, "Well, it will come, probably in about nine months. And I'll try to warn you about it, but you won't pay any attention to me."

I left John's office thinking, This guy's a nut!

I worked long, hard hours trying to transform the street kids of Hackney. The work I did was face-to-face youth work. The kids were very needy, and they were generally in my home 24/7. I had no clue about how to set up boundaries, so my experience was probably hyperrelational. Some good things took place. Many of the kids

came to faith. Kids came out of the gangs and out of their violent
and difficult backgrounds and into the kingdom. To this day many
of them are in full-time ministry. It was a wonderful time, a fantastic
place to be. But I had a lot to learn.

Then it finally happened. One morning, about nine months after my
conversation with John, I woke up exhausted. I'd had a full night's
sleep, but I felt more tired getting up in the morning than I had going
to bed. For months and months I had worked endless hours trying
to produce what I perceived to be a fruitful ministry. That morning I
realized I neglected practically every other part of my life in a grand
effort to change as many lives as possible in the name of the Lord.
But it was that morning when I realized that I had nothing left in
my physical or spiritual fuel tank to offer anyone. I was completely
burned out.

> SADLY, IN OUR
> BUSYNESS, WE
> END UP DAMAGING
> THE VERY
> RELATIONSHIPS
> WE ARE TRYING
> SO HARD TO
> MAINTAIN.

I looked at my face in the mirror and
saw an old man staring back at me. I
was only twenty-one, not old and worn
out like that guy. How did he get in my
bathroom? Although I couldn't think
straight, I knew that I was in trouble
and had no idea how to get out. I
burst into tears. It was my feelings of
foolishness, inadequacy, and guilt that
led to my burnout. I had taken the
entire responsibility of ministry onto
my own shoulders, rather than allowing
God to take on the burden, and the weight had become too much
for me to bear. God had become a participant in my plan rather
than me being a participant in his. I have seen this kind of behavior
lead people to such a burnout that they have been hospitalized for
nervous breakdowns. It has also led to such dangerous circumstances
that pastors have quit ministry altogether because they grew so

disenfranchised. Fortunately, I was not in *that* much trouble, but I was walking a fine line. I had to get away.

When John opened his door to see me standing there, he didn't need any explanation. He didn't even invite me in. He just looked at me and said, "Wait there."

John returned with the envelope that he'd shown me nine months earlier and handed it to me.

"Now's not the time to talk," he said. "Take the money and use it to get a train ride home. Take as long as you need to get some rest. Sleep, eat, whatever. When you're refreshed, come back, and then we'll talk."

I went home to Sheffield. My parents were moving to a new house, so I slept on Sally's living room floor for two weeks. Every day, all day, I would ride around Sheffield. I sat at the top of a double-decker bus, just staring out the window, often with tears streaming down my face. It was the space I needed to allow my heart to heal and for my life to be put back together again.

The problem was that I had believed that my success as a youth pastor depended on how much I did and what I did. I didn't take the time to look at what God was doing or even how he wanted things done. I'd been determined to do it all for him.

I made a decision that I was going to find a way to live differently. I've never burned out to that extreme again, but there have been other occasions in my life when my passion to get something done for the Lord has nearly driven me to the edge of breakdown. During those times, God would tell me again and again, "Let me do it." One time I actually set myself on fire in my backyard. That's what it took for God to get my attention.[1] I was able to learn from that experience and it changed my life. I came to grips with what God meant when he said, "Let me do it."

FAST-FORWARD TWENTY YEARS

Over the past thirty years that it's taken me to develop LifeShapes, I have seen and worked with many Christians who are so busy doing for God that they have nothing left to give. Sadly, in our busyness, we end up damaging the very relationships we are trying so hard to maintain. We feel like failures because we are unable (both physically and emotionally) to keep up. Across the country, ministries and churches are on the verge of collapse as well. Despite all their work and effort, their reach is ineffectual and unproductive. Why? Because they are exhausted and burned out. How long before they close their doors forever?

The rhythm of our lives (perpetuated by our culture) is completely opposite of the rhythm that God designed for our well-being. It is crucial that we rediscover God's rhythm for mankind. The Semi-Circle, the second shape in the *LifeShapes* series, challenges us to order our lives according to the way that Jesus taught his disciples. As disciples of Jesus, we need to rediscover from Scripture how to live fruitful lives of balance: work from rest, rest from work. When we do, we're overjoyed to discover that God takes over. No longer stressed and overwhelmed, life falls into place in a wonderful new way.

How does this take shape? While it's true that we must all come to a point where we are willing to say, "Let God do it," in order for God

---

1.   You can read this story in the LifeShapes book about the Circle, *Choosing to Learn from Life*.

to take control we must still take the first step.

Before we get into the Semi-Circle, take a few minutes to reflect on your own definitions of work and rest, fruitfulness and abiding in the Lord.

- What does productivity mean to you?
- How do you define success in your career, ministry, and in your family life?
- What kinds of adventures and retreats characterize your life?
- How do you spend time with the Lord?

Reflecting upon your answers to these questions will prepare you for what is to come in the following chapters, and indeed, your answers will prove significant to your own life.

As you read on, I will challenge the way you and I live in today's fast paced, gadget-driven society. God's rhythm for our lives has biblical basis that even I, a trained pastor in the ministry, had missed for many years. Don't let this happen to you! The life application of the Semi-Circle principle is simple and life changing. I invite you to discover its truth for yourself.

CHAPTER 1

ENOUGH IS ENOUGH

S ome years ago in England, writer and critic Clive James hosted a television show.[2] He used to show clips of foreign television programs, particularly a Japanese show called "Endurance." Contestants submitted themselves to intense and unbelievable forms of pressure or torture: gooey stuff, painful stuff, smelly stuff, maggoty stuff, humiliating stuff. Viewers would catch their breath, and across the nation you'd hear, "Eew!"

Sometimes after showing the clip, Clive James wouldn't even comment. The clip had said enough. What more was there to say about people who would willingly subject themselves to stomach turning circumstances just to win a prize? This was no way to live.

---

2. *Saturday Night Clive*, (London, England: ITV1, 1998).

WHY IS IT SO
ENTERTAINING TO
WATCH PEOPLE
LOSE, SUFFER,
BREAK DOWN, AND
CRY?

Now jump ahead a few years. You may not have heard of Clive James or the Japanese television show he featured, but other images are certainly coming to your mind—images from American television on multiple networks. We see it on TV all the time. People compete to be part of a band, face their darkest fears, stick their faces into unimaginable substances, tear each other apart in front of a national audience for a job, endure demanding primitive conditions in some distant part of the world. All to win the prize.

And the thing is, we love it. Many of us who would never do those things ourselves nevertheless are mesmerized by watching others do them. Bizarre as they are, something about these programs is entertaining and compelling. From our recliners and couches we root for people to win battles that seem absurd to fight in the first place. Our own heart rates and blood pressures rise as we watch people we've never heard of before put themselves through these experiences.

Why is it so entertaining to watch people lose, suffer, break down, and cry? And why do the winners receive their fifteen minutes of fame when they win?

I believe we have our own twenty-first-century version of the gladiator games of ancient Rome. In Roman times gladiator games were hugely popular. A day at the games began with watching fighters battle against animals in the mornings. Over lunch people watched the executions of convicted criminals (this was also the time of day that the Christians were executed during times of persecution). In the afternoon, viewers saw their gladiator heroes fight one another to the death.

It seems that today we still look for heroes who can win impossible battles against impossible odds. No matter how contrived some of these shows are, they call it "reality TV" for a reason. We may not be racing around the world or sticking our faces in buckets of goop, but when we watch these shows we empathize, recognizing the impossible battles we ourselves face, the stresses and strains of everyday life that bring us to the breaking point. The backdrop may be

different, but we understand the pressure of trying to get hired, finding a life partner, raising a family, pursuing a dream. We feel reassured when we see other people break the way that we break and fear what we fear. For a moment we can forget and don't have to deal with our own stress. Perhaps it even gives us hope that, like our ordinary heroes, we too can overcome.

But does it tell us something else? Does reality television reveal that in some ways our society is as depraved as that of the gladiator world? The gladiators might have been heroes, but why get in the ring with a pack of lions in the first place? Let's think through what twenty-first-century battles look like in our everyday life.

> WE FEEL REASSURED WHEN WE SEE OTHER PEOPLE BREAK THE WAY THAT WE BREAK AND FEAR WHAT WE FEAR.

COMPETING TO STAY AHEAD

The reasons why may be hard to describe, but there's no disputing that we are a society that doesn't seem to know when to stop working. We are productive, yet we want to produce more. Americans are working harder than ever. Research from The Families and Work Institute says that one in three Americans is chronically

overworked,[3] and a more recent study by ABC shows that more than
half of all American's feel overworked and overwhelmed.[4] We've all
bought into the idea that technology will make life so much easier.
We have smart phones, tablets, email, text messages, the Internet...
All of these have made the world a smaller place. Sometimes we
wonder how we ever managed without them. But I assure you, we
once did.

The downside is that technology also makes it easier to keep on
working. The office can always be with you now. It follows you in
your ever lengthening commute when you move out to the suburbs
for an affordable home. It stays with you through the evening when
you are trying to relax. You can work until midnight if you want.
Sometimes you do. And why wouldn't you? Everybody's doing it.
It's what you need to do to stay ahead, to show you are focused and
committed. Everyone knows that jobs are not as secure as they used
to be, especially now that so many are being outsourced to different
parts of the world. Despite the efficiencies of technology, we're
working longer hours than we did fifty years ago—even more than
medieval peasants. Fourteen percent of Americans are holding down
two or more jobs just to stay on top of things.[5] You've got a family to
provide for; you do what you have to.

Sound familiar?

When it comes to time off, most Americans get about two weeks
of vacation a year, though many get no paid vacation at all.
(Interestingly, European workers receive an average of five or six
weeks of vacation time a year.) According to a recent article in the

---

3. Families and Work Institute, *Overwork in America: When the Way We Work Becomes Too
    Much*, Executive Summary, 2005, http://www.familiesandwork.org.
4. Study: *US Workers Burned Out*, http://abcnews.go.com/US/story?id=93295
5. Ibid.

Huffington Post, fourty seven percent of American employees did not take any vacation days in 2014.[6] They save those days for when they are ill or can't find day care; or they feel that being away from work would just put them too far behind to be worth it.

Ever been there?

Most of us have. It's one of the battles that we face every day. It's a fight to stay ahead if we want to achieve our goals, pursue our dreams. So we work harder and harder, competing with others privately—or even publicly—on how many hours we spend working. The hero is the one who manages to do the most.

FAMILY LIFE

This battle isn't just being waged at work.

Studies show that younger Gen X and Gen Y workers (defined as those born between 1965 and 1994) are more likely to prioritize family life, or at least aim to give family and work equal footing.[7] This is a change from their boomer parents, who often put work first at a high price to the family. But it's not that the younger generations work fewer hours; rather, they try to fit more into the time they don't have! Life at home needs organization and it is at least as tiring and demanding as the office. We want it all, so we bring home the same high expectations we impose on ourselves at work. Obviously, we must have the perfect home, drive the right car, send our kids to the

---

6. Leigh Weingus, *Way Too Many Americans Took ZERO Vacation Days In 2014*, Huffington Post, 2015, http://www.huffingtonpost.com/2015/01/05/americans-vacation-days-2014_n_6419100.html
7. Amy Joyce, *Gen Xers Not Lazy But Have Eyes on a Different Prize*. Milwaukee Journal Sentinel, December 15, 2004, http://www.jsonline.com/bym/career/dec04/284041.asp.

right camps and sports clubs. We must earn the kind of money that provides the lifestyle that we want to display.

When all is said and done, people have no time to relax. They have no time to form significant friendships, to spend time with spouses, no time to talk and hang out with their kids. It's affecting everything, including our health. Studies show that the vast majority of visits to the physician are for stress related illnesses.[8] We are always on the move, so there is no time for a lunch break; we fly past the vending machine and grab a candy bar just to stop the stomach from gurgling for a while. The evening is packed with activity; by the time we have a chance to eat, we leap at something fast—most likely high calorie and unhealthy. This trend of unhealthy eating and exercise habits has revealed that more than one third of children and adolescents are overweight or obese.

Furthering the health crisis for our kids is the rise in the diagnosis of Type 2 diabetes in children and adolescents, which can increase the lifetime risk for many serious chronic diseases.[9]

Who is the hero in all this?

The Super Mom? The Soccer Mom? The Little League Dad? At least from a distance, they seem to be able to hold it all together. But how are they attempting to do it? In November of 2012 the US Centers for Disease Control and Prevention (CDC) showed that eleven percent of Americans 12 and older use Prozac, Zoloft, Paxil or other antidepressants.[10] And when the antidepressants don't do the trick,

---

8. Kevin Lamb, "Sickness Can Be Price of Unbridled Stress", *MindBodyHealth*, May 22, 2005, http://www.mindbodyhealth.com/stressillness.htm.
9. Institute of Medicine of the National Academies, *Childhood Obesity in the United States: Facts and Figures*. Fact Sheet, September 2004, http://www.iom.edu.
10. http://www.cdc.gov/nchs/data/databriefs/db76.htm

divorce is often the next answer. According to American Community Survey (ACS) and Decennial Census data, 35% of children under 18 live in single parent families.[11]

MINI-ME

Our kids often get as burned out as we do. We want them to do well in life, to be prepared to thrive in the cutthroat world in which we find ourselves. So we feel we have to provide opportunities for them to learn the skills they'll need.

But the competition begins so early on. You hear the stories of infants listening to classical music in the crib or in the womb—not necessarily because their parents like it, but because a study says Mozart will stimulate an infant's mental ability. We can't just hand children toys and let them explore and make discoveries about the world anymore. We have to know in advance precisely what the children will learn from each toy. Prereading skills? Premath skills? Social skills? Language skills?

Competition is fierce beginning as early as the preschool level. As children grow older, on top of their homework requirements they are also involved in activity after activity—classes that will improve their skills, set them up for life, help their development; sports that will help them realize their potential. Who knows, your child could be the next Tiger Woods, or you could be raising the next Williams sisters. They need to stay ahead. After all, they are the heroes of tomorrow.

---

11. http://datacenter.kidscount.org/data/tables/106-children-in-single-parent-families

What is the effect of all this pressure—and not teaching the value of rest—on our kids? Let me tell you:

> Some estimates place the number as high as 6 percent of young women who become pregnant *at least once* before they reach the age of twenty.[12]

> When teens perceive problems to be outside their control, they often turn to suicide—the third leading cause of death among young people aged fifteen to twenty-four.[13]

> The common denominator to both of these problems is teen alcohol abuse. The average age when youth first try alcohol is eleven for boys and thirteen for girls. If they do start drinking before age fifteen, they're five times more likely to develop alcohol dependence than those who start at the age of twenty-one.[14]

In fact, the Girl Scouts now have a "Stress Less" merit badge, the purpose of which is to equip young girls to deal with the pressures of life. You may laugh, but once upon a time no one would have considered such a thing necessary for children. It appears we all feel overworked, and family life is suffering.

Fortunately, not everyone is convinced. Not everyone wants to be a hero. Some people just want their lives back, their families back. And they are telling people to get out of the gladiator's ring. They see beyond the occasional hero who on the surface seems to have it all together. They see the countless everyday casualties who just don't make it.

---

12. www.thenationalcampaign.org/data/compare/1678
13. www.cdc.gov/nchs/data/databriefs/db37.htm
14. www.cdc.gov/alcohol/fact-sheets/underage-drinking.htm

Take Back Your Time is an American and Canadian initiative created to challenge what is seen as "the epidemic of overwork, over scheduling, and time famine that now threatens our health, our families and relationships, our communities, and our environment."[15] Organizations like this campaign for new ways of living such as longer vacations, paid sick leave, guaranteed paid childbirth leave for all parents, and limits to mandatory overtime.

Another positive trendsetter is the community of Ridgewood, New Jersey, which set up "Ready, Set, Relax!" This is a time when sports events, homework, and religious classes were canceled for the evening so that people could spend time with their families.[16] Harvard's dean of admis- sions, William Fitzsimmons, encourages incoming students to take a year off before college to pursue something com- pletely different.[17] Countless books, talk-show hosts, and classes are available that encourage us to take a deep breath and take back our lives.

And then there are the Christians like you and me.

THROWN TO THE LIONS?

Today's gladiator games are no different for Christians. In fact, we're usually devoured by lunchtime.

Research by the Barna Group on Christians and stress reveals many opinions on the work-family-church balance. George Barna says that American Christians still struggle to reconcile Christian teachings and the desire to lead healthy, low-stress lives. They wonder whether

---

15. www.timeday.org
16. Sonja Steptoe, "Ready, Set, Relax!" *Time*, October 27, 2003.
17. Brian Braiker, "Time Off Helps," *Newsweek*, Kaplan College Guide, 2005 edition.

the two fit together. His research shows that many Christians believe hard work, competition in the workplace, and aggressive financial strategies are compatible with being a Christian. Other Christians feel that their education, financial status, and active lifestyle communicate their faith.[18]

We feel called to be good employees; it's a part of our wit- ness. So we will work at least as hard as our colleagues, smiling all the while. We know our call is to be a good friend, spouse, child, or parent. So we work hard to make sure the people we care about have all they need and that when we spend time with them, it's "quality" time. And of course we know we are called to be active in the lives of our churches. So added to the pressures of work and family life, there are the numerous church activities in which we want to be involved, so we search for ways we can volunteer. We know that having a relationship with God is crucial, so we will try and fit him in somewhere, trying not to feel too guilty for how bad we are at holding to our quiet times.

> WE SOMEHOW FEEL MORE HOLY IF WE ARE DOING MORE FOR GOD.

But we rarely hear the cry to get out of the ring; trying to meet all these expectations is too important. Instead, we think that we need to become better gladiators, super-Christians who manage to have it all and succeed. Somehow we feel like better people if we juggle everything and stay on top of things, even if only temporarily. Rather than being counter cultural, as Christians should, we spiritualize the busyness. We somehow feel more holy if we are doing more for God. We try to please him in the same ways that we live to please others.

---

18. The Barna Group, "Views on Quality of Life Are Most Influenced by Money and Faith," April 24, 2003, www.barna.org/FlexPage.aspx?Page=BarnaUpdate&BarnaUpdateID=137.

If we are honest with ourselves, we know that the pace of life is devouring us just like it is everyone else. It's all too much. Some studies show that *every month* more than one thousand pastors leave their jobs.[19] They can't continue with the round-the-clock approach to work and ministry. Their families can't cope with it either.

Sadly, Barna's research shows that being a Christian doesn't provide any insurance that your marriage has a better chance of lasting. Whether respondents classified themselves as born-again Christians or non-Christians, the divorce rate was the same: 33 percent.[20] What we as Christians are doing right now isn't enough. We need to separate ourselves more and live like Jesus teaches us.

> Has it gotten to be too much for you yet?
> Do you find it hard to say no?
> How many hours do you work each week?
> How much of your vacation have you taken?
> Do you resent spending time with your friends or family?
> Do you know how to turn off your smart phone at the end of the working day?
> Do your kids need to be involved in every activity?
> Do you carve out time to spend with God?

Jesus said that he came that we should have life, and have it to the fullest. But full doesn't always have to mean *busy*.

---

19. Kings and Priests, "Statistics About Pastors," www.kings-priests.org/priests.php

20. The Barna Group, "New Marriage and Divorce Statistics Released," March 31, 2008, www.barna.org/barna-update/family-kids/42-new-marriage-and-divorce-statistics-released

ANOTHER KIND OF HERO?

In the film *Gladiator*[21], a remarkable hero named Maximus comes to the fore. His concern is not winning the battles in the ring, but defeating the power behind the empire: Commodus. In the end, he gives his life for freedom—the physical freedom of the slaves who Maximus fought alongside and freedom for the Roman people from the tyranny and the corruption that ate away at the heart of their community.

Rather than trying to cope with the pressures of our world and trying to be the hero at the cost of our lives, perhaps it's time to look at things another way.

Maybe it is time to be freed from the bondage of living this way, and the feeling that we need to live this way. We need to get out of the ring. We need to see that the way we live may tell us something deeper about ourselves and our walk with God. This lifestyle isn't healthy; we need to change.

It's not hard to see the parallels. As Christians we responded to one who gave his life so that we too could be free. Jesus rose up and defeated the powers that had a grip on our world so that we could live differently. He offered us life in all its fullness.

Now that you've seen the statistics and understand the results of an unbalanced rhythm of life, what can you realistically do about it? Jesus taught us that life—real, true, *abundant* life—only comes as a result of living in the natural rhythm with which we were originally created. As we will discover in the following chapters, the Semi-Circle

---

21. *Gladiator*, DVD, directed by Ridley Scott (England, Morocco, Malta: Universal Pictures and Dreamworks, 2000).

works well for depicting this rhythm, because the sweeping back and forth of the pendulum creates the image of a Semi-Circle.

Jesus is the same yesterday, today, and tomorrow. That means he's doing the same things with us today as he did with his first disciples. He's teaching us, training us, helping us to be more like him every day. He truly wants to help us balance work and rest as he successfully did during his time on earth.

As Christians we've decided that Jesus is a Savior worth following. So what does the freedom that he gives us look like? And is it relevant to our everyday, overstressed, pressured lives?

We're going to take a walk with Jesus and his disciples and explore the deeper meaning within one of Jesus' final and most beautiful parables. A parable whose truths, when revealed to us in our busy lives, can have the power to change us and restore the balance and tranquility we so desperately crave.

CHAPTER 2

A DIFFERENT KIND OF RHYTHM

Key Word

Abiding:
*Drawing near to Jesus so that you become aware of his love for you
and his word to you.*

Picture in your mind the final evening Jesus shared his teaching with his disciples. It was Thursday night. Jesus and his disciples spent the evening in an upper room. Jerusalem, like any other city in Israel at the time, had many homes with accommodations for pilgrims who came at feast times. This form of hospitality was part of the culture of the Jewish people. Usually this room was the last part of the house to be built, after the family's most pressing needs had been met. Often the room was built on the roof of the house, thus called an "upper room."

Jesus and his disciples had eaten; perhaps they prepared the food over a grill on the roof. Because it was Passover, this night was different from the other times they had been together for a meal. With common bread and wine, Jesus conducted a brief service that we now call the "Lord's Supper." The disciples were still baffled by Jesus' talk of going away. Jesus earlier had sent Judas to do what was in his heart to do. Not much time was left, and Jesus still had some things to say to his disciples—his closest friends.

When they had finished eating, Jesus and his disciples left the upper room. "Come on, guys, let's get out of here." No, Jesus is not leading his disciples on a fast getaway. He's just letting them know that they're finished in that place. They have other things to do somewhere else. It's time to move on. They walked across the roof and down the stairs into the streets of Jerusalem. Hundreds of thousands of people had arrived in Jerusalem for Passover, so the streets were teeming with commotion and hub-bub. The smell of lambs roasting over cooking fires permeated the air. As they passed by homes, Jesus and the disciples soaked up the sounds of people singing and speaking psalms.

They navigated through the crowded streets on their way to their campsite, the place they favored when they came to Jerusalem, the place where Jesus liked to go (in fact, Luke tells us they often went there). It is up on the Mount of Olives in a garden called Gethsemane. On their way to the Mount of Olives, they walked past the Temple Mount. The temple of the living God is an absolute wonder of architecture and art. It was impossible for the disciples to walk past it without lifting their eyes to its splendor.

The vision was breathtaking. The temple rose proudly, built from white marble extracted from the best mines around the world. Its beauty was illuminated by the thousands of oil flames in the hundreds of homes in the area, and by the great candelabra that stood in the temple courtyard. Around the parapet of the temple, carved into the white marble, overlaid with gold and silver given by men of great wealth around the world, was the symbol of Israel. This symbol, drawn from Psalm 80, is one that every Jewish person understands as the image of the people of God. It is a vine.

> You brought a vine out of Egypt;
> you drove out the nations and planted it.
> You cleared the ground for it, and it took root and
> filled the land.
>
> —Psalm 80:8–9

Jesus paused, turned to his disciples, and said,

> I am the true vine, and my Father is the gardener.... You
> are the branches.
>
> —John 15:1, 5

He kept walking, down the hill and through the Kidron valley. Ahead of him were olive groves, and on his right was a vineyard. As he walked past the vineyard, Jesus continued,

> I am the true vine, and my Father is the gardener. He cuts off every branch in me that bears no fruit, while every branch that does bear fruit he trims clean so that it will be even more fruitful. You are already clean because of the word I have spoken to you. Remain in me, and I will remain in you. No branch can bear fruit by itself; it must remain in the vine. Neither can you bear fruit unless you remain in me.

> I am the vine; you are the branches. If a man remains in me and I in him, he will bear much fruit; apart from me you can do nothing. If anyone does not remain in me, he is like a branch that is thrown away and withers; such branches are picked up, thrown into the fire and burned. If you remain in me and my words remain in you, ask whatever you wish, and it will be given you. This is to my Father's glory, that you bear much fruit, showing yourselves to be my disciples.
>
> —John 15:1-8

The disciples were accustomed to Jesus using pictures and parables to better illustrate the kingdom of God to them. This subject matter was particularly significant, though. The image of the vine was at the heart of every Israelite, at the core of their identity as a people. Part of the symbolism of being a Jew in the first century was to grow your own fig tree and your own vine. The disciples would have been familiar with how vines grew and the significance of what Jesus was saying. Jesus took the time to share something vitally important with his disciples at a crucial time—the night before his crucifixion. We (unlike those first disciples) know what is about to happen when Jesus arrives in Gethsemane. We know why Judas left supper early and how events are about to unfold. Yet Jesus took the time to go into great detail with this parable.

I come from a military family, which is why I tend to be a bit of a neat freak. Any military person will tell you that the last word is always the most important. If you're on parade and the sergeant major dresses you down and tells you what a terrible soldier you are, the very last command he gives is the thing that you do. If he says, "attention," then you come to attention. If he says, "at ease," then you stand at ease. The last order is the most important, because the last thing is the first thing that you should do.

The image of the vine is the last parable or picture that Jesus gave us. It's reasonable for us to assume that this is a tremendously important picture for us to understand. Perhaps it's even the most fundamental image from among all the pictures that he gave us. Jesus was trying to get the attention of his disciples, both then and today.

But we twenty-first-century disciples, especially those of us who have grown up in more urban settings, need a more complete explanation of this parable. What exactly is Jesus talking about?

VINE GROWING 101

> I am the vine; you are the branches. If a man remains in
> me and I in him, he will bear much fruit.
>
> —John 15:5

The disciples, like everyone in Israel, knew how to grow vines. You
plant a new vine—and then you keep cutting it back, pruning it
brutally. The vine is not allowed to bear fruit for three years, not even
flowers, not even a leaf. All you can see is a thick, stocky trunk, the
vine itself.

After those first three years, the vine is finally allowed to grow and
produce fruit. It is now ready for a pattern of growth and harvest,
growth and harvest. After the harvest you cut back all the branches of
the vine, both the fruitful and the dead branches, pruning to within
just a couple millimeters of the vine itself. The central plant, which
grows to about eighteen inches high, will look like it has died.

Yet the disciples also knew that over the slow growing months of
winter the vine would grow around the pruned branches and the
branches would seem to disappear. The branches will abide in the
vine. They will be in the vine, hidden from normal observation. All
anyone can see is a curious looking stump. When the growing season
of early spring arrives, green shoots begin to emerge from the places
where the branches have been. You'll set up a trellis behind the vine
to support these green shoots, or set sticks in the dirt like crutches to
hold them up.

As they grow on these supports, the branches come into blossom and
then bear fruit. The thing about a vine is that if you leave the fruit
on the branch, it will remain. The fruit is allowed to stay on the vine
branch because this is the kind of fruit that lasts, fruit that abides,

fruit that remains. It's not like fruit on an apple tree. Westerners know that if you leave apples on the tree, eventually they will rot and drop. But Jesus is talking about fruit on a vine. You can leave this fruit there for months because it is fruit that lasts.

As soon as you pick the fruit, you prune the branches back until they are virtually invisible. Once again, during the slow growing months of winter, the vine grows around the pruned branches, and the branches abide in the vine. Soon enough it will be spring and the cycle will repeat again. This is the pattern of growth and pruning.

THE RHYTHM OF LIFE

When a pendulum swings in rhythm, back and forth, to and fro, it creates the pattern of a Semi-Circle. In this final parable from Jesus before he goes to the cross, Jesus outlines the pattern of life for all of his disciples. It is a rhythmic pattern, back and forth, to and fro. At one end of the pendulum's arc is **abiding**; at the other end is **fruitfulness**.

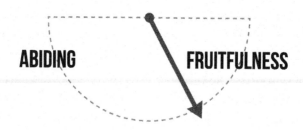

In this passage, the New International Version uses the word "remain." Older translations of the Bible, such as the King James Version, use the word "abide." I like the word "abide." It evokes what Jesus was trying to describe. He said, "The branch needs to abide in the vine. And if it abides in the vine, then it will bear much fruit." So, here's the pattern:

Abiding

Growing

Bearing fruit

Pruning

Now, for all you Bible scholars, it's true that the word "growing" does not appear in the text. But it's obviously implied. It's difficult to get from abiding to producing fruit without growing somewhere in the process.

This pattern, this rhythm, reflects God's plan for our lives. This is how he has designed us to live. I assert that this is the biblical alternative to the overworked, overstressed rat race we often find ourselves in. Jesus points his disciples to a practical pattern of life that is radically different—one that can work well in our culture.

ABIDE WITH ME

> Remain in me, and I will remain in you. No branch can bear fruit by itself; it must remain in the vine. Neither can you bear fruit unless you remain in me.
>
> —John 15:4

The first thing we discover when we look closely at God's rhythm for our lives is that it starts at a completely different place from what we would expect. We often begin with frenzied activity. We plan our schedules with as much as we can get done in the time that we have. We fill in every square on the calendar, every line in the planner. We work as hard as we can all week, hoping to get a break on the weekend. Some of us don't ever get a break; we are busy catching up with things around the house or taking children to various activities, or even catching up on work we didn't finish during the week. And we haven't even mentioned church activities yet! Instead of resting, we're simply busy doing something else. Before we know it, it's Monday morning and the craziness begins all over again. And we're exhausted.

> WE NEED JESUS' WORDS TO GO DOWN DEEP WITHIN OUR HEARTS, BUT THAT CAN'T HAPPEN WHEN LIFE IS TOO BUSY TO HEAR HIM.

Disciples of Jesus are called to dance to the beat of a different drum, and that dance begins with abiding. Jesus invites us to abide in him, to abide in his love, to let his words abide in us.

What does Jesus mean when he says, "Abide in me"?

Let's go back to the picture of the vine and the branches. When the branches start out, they are kept close to the vine. The vine surrounds and protects the branches through the harsh winter.

To abide in Jesus means to stay close to him, be with him, to let him surround our lives the same way the vine surrounds the branches. Jesus knows that we branches are vulnerable to the elements of the world around us. The pressure, the stress and strain of everyday life can break even the strongest branch. The only way to get to a place where we can be fruitful is to stay close to the vine.

We need Jesus' words to go down deep within our hearts, but that can't happen when life is too busy to hear him. We need to stay close to Jesus so that we are reminded every day of his unconditional love, his gift of grace to us. His love gives us a security through life that the world and all its expectations can't possibly provide.

GOD WANTS OUR COMPANY

As a pastor, I have often found that the summer months are the best time to abide. I try to make space in my calendar to hang out with Jesus. I spend time reading the Bible. I talk to him through the day. I play golf with him. It's not that I don't have everyday activities to attend to; I am still a pastor, husband, and father. Abiding doesn't mean I go into hiding for eight weeks. But my life has a noticeably different pace to it.

Abiding is not just for individuals. We abide as a family, taking time to be together. We also have abiding seasons as a church. When I was a pastor at St. Thomas' Church in England, the staff team abode during the summer vacation months of July and August. They worked half days. The rest of the time they spent with their families or their friends. Our weekend services took on a more relaxed feel, with a simple time of singing and a brief word of encouragement. Everything was about abiding in Jesus, allowing him to surround us with his love. Even though I am no longer at St. Thomas', the staff and many of the church members continue to exercise a time of abiding during the summer months.

In the coming chapters, you are going to hear from some close friends of the Breen family, Mark and Penny Carey. When they first came to Sheffield to lead a new church, it was clear that their priorities of work and rest, fruitfulness and abiding, were not in balance. They had a toddler, a baby, a ministry, and a marriage to balance. Like most of us, they were taught that life was measured in terms of their achievements; that a good day was a busy day. They both came from backgrounds demanding a strong work ethic. And that strong ethic always made them feel guilty about taking time off.

Everything changed when they first learned about the Semi-Circle. They started to understand that while a strong work ethic was a good thing, it became unhealthy when it started to rule their lives. As they gained sight of the fact that they needed to take time to rest, they began to lead fruitful and abundant lives that were balanced and refreshing. They have spent years practicing the rhythm of life and they have some fantastic examples that are practical and easy for anyone to adopt into his or her own life of abiding and resting. As you listen to Mark's story, take a moment to consider if you are making the time to abide in Jesus.

> Making time for God has sometimes been hard for me, and I know I'm not the only one. I'm an activist at heart and have the kind of personality that "needs to be needed." I struggle with abiding in Jesus because it doesn't feel active enough. After all, what am I actually doing? I've had to remind myself of the high value Jesus himself put on cultivating an abiding relationship with the Father. As his disciple, I am learning to do the same. I have come to understand that the Lord wants my company. The word "company" comes from an old French word compagnie, meaning "eating bread together." There is something very ordinary about this relationship, an everyday relationship of intimacy that is life giving and not life sapping.

> —Mark

Sometimes we are too busy trying to get things done for God. We try to show him that we are committed, that we love him. But we can get so busy with activity for Jesus that we miss out on simply abiding with him. He wants to speak to you and be close to you. He wants to hang out with you as you work, raise your kids, or spend time with friends. You must realize that he simply wants to enjoy your company. Where do you go or spend time that you could invite God along? What could abiding look like for you from here on out? For your family? For your small group? For your church?

Abiding is the key to growing and becoming fruitful. Do you ever experience those moments in your life where you are constantly asking yourself why all your hard work isn't paying off? Or do you find yourself relentlessly trying to be fruitful in your career, your home life, your ministry, or even your hobbies without seeing any tangible results? If you are always attempting to grow and multiply the fruits of your labor without taking the time to abide, I can assure you that nothing significant is going to happen in the goals that you have set for your life. Once you learn that work and rest, fruitfulness and abiding are a process that requires balance, you will begin to see the patterns that God has determined for your life. Once you learn to rest and abide, God will reveal the amazing ways in which you can grow and be fruitful.

CHAPTER 3

GROWING IN GOD

Key Words

Growing:
*Developing, maturing, and making progress on the journey
to which God has called you.*

Bearing Fruit:
*Multiplying the life that is within us. We ask that the life of Jesus
in us be reproduced in the lives of others.*

Pruning:
*Surrendering to God's call to stop what we are doing
and start returning to him.*

A s you learn to abide in the vine by spending time with Jesus, you will start to notice patterns of fruitfulness and growth in your life. Let's face the facts: We were never designed to be fruit ful all the time. But you will soon discover how fruitful you can be following a time of rest and abiding with the Lord. Although growing is not directly mentioned in John 15, it is the automatic result of time spent abiding. After three years of abiding, the branches on the vine are allowed to grow. And because these branches are still attached to the vine, they are strong enough for the grapes, or fruit, that are about to come.

The same is true for us. Abiding in Jesus helps us to grow spiritually. His love and his words nurture us and strengthen us when we allow him to surround our lives. Time spent in worship, daily prayer, or Bible reading is a wonderful way to abide in Jesus.

> IT'S TEMPTING TO JUST TRY HARDER WHEN IT FEELS LIKE NOTHING IS HAPPENING. BUT JESUS SHOWS US THAT GROWTH BEGINS WITH HIM, NOT US. IT STARTS WITH ABIDING.

Are you growing spiritually?

Are you seeing more of Jesus working in your life, your family, your friendships, your church?

It's tempting to just try harder when it feels like nothing is happening. But Jesus shows us that growth begins with him, not us. It starts with abiding.

BEARING FRUIT

> I am the vine; you are the branches. If a man remains in me and I in him, he will bear much fruit; apart from me you can do nothing.
>
> —John 15:5

Now here's the exciting part: Fruitfulness is the most natural thing for a branch. It doesn't have to strain to produce grapes. Fruitfulness happens quite naturally.

The first disciples spent three years hanging out with Jesus. Coincidence? They spent time with him, listened to him, and learned from him. They were probably wondering when they would get the chance to get into what they had signed up to do. Whether they realized it or not, they were in the midst of the abiding and growing cycle. Six weeks after Jesus gave them the picture of the vine, the disciples' ministry would suddenly burst out in fruitfulness.

> This is to my Father's glory, that you bear much fruit, showing yourselves to be my disciples.
>
> —John 15:8

On the day of Pentecost, empow- ered by the Holy Spirit, the disciples preached to the gathered crowds. Three thousand people became Christians in one day (see Acts 2:41). After three years of what seemed like small amounts of fruit, the disciples' baskets were overflowing.

> You did not choose me, but I chose you to go and bear fruit—fruit that will last.
>
> —John 15:16

The disciples not only were fruitful in the number of lives they touched, but also in the way they lived their lives. Their community was known as "The Way" because the group acted, lived, and thought in a particular way. The community of Jesus was marked by the values that Jesus lived and taught among them. They loved one another, shared their possessions, met together daily praising God and praying. They

> THE DISCIPLES NOT ONLY WERE FRUITFUL IN THE NUMBER OF LIVES THEY TOUCHED, BUT ALSO IN THE WAY THEY LIVED THEIR LIVES.

broke bread together, as Jesus had taught them to do. And the city of Jerusalem was shaken by these gentle revolutionaries who were beginning to change the world forever.

So what does fruit look like for us today?

The fruit of a plant is actually its means of reproduction. Fruit enables the multiplication of the DNA of a particular organism. One example of fruitful living is when Jesus told his disciples to love one another in the way that he had loved them (see John 15:12). Love was at the heart of the early church's lifestyle. And it spread.

But the simplest way to understand fruitfulness in our con- text is that Jesus has multiplied himself into the lives of the disciples and he expects the disciples to multiply their lives into other people. That is the most direct understanding of what Jesus is talking about. We have so often defined fruitful- ness as directly leading others to become Christians—guiding them through the prayer of salvation. This places a lot of pres- sure on believers (which I elaborate on in the context of the *LifeShapes* book about the Octagon, *Living Life with a Mission*). The Great Commission is about making disciples—*learners*—of Jesus. Perhaps your role is simply planting a seed for others to harvest later.

So when we consider what it means to be fruitful, we have to ask ourselves,

- Do I reproduce the life of Jesus in the life of others?

To put it more bluntly,

- Have I taught anyone about living the life of Jesus through my life?
- Have friends or colleagues witnessed this through my living?
- Is the love that Jesus expressed for me being reproduced in my family?

- Do we have healthy relationships with one another?"
- When I am with other Christians, do we reproduce the community of Jesus?
- Are we good to be around?
- Are we people who love and care for each other in practical ways?
- Do people see something different in our community?
- Love instead of unforgiveness?
- Sharing our possessions instead of competing and comparing ourselves?
- Genuine, uplifting friendship instead of superficial relationships?

How fruitful are you? In other words, is your life produc- tive? Is it effective and successful? Does bearing fruit come naturally to you, or do you feel like you are straining to produce the occasional grape? If we are not seeing any of these things in our lives, then we need to ask ourselves why.

PRUNING

The next stage in life on the vine is perhaps the hardest for us to understand.

> I am the true vine and my Father is the gar- dener. He cuts off every branch in me that bears no fruit, while every branch that does bear fruit he trims clean so that it will be even more fruitful.
>
> —John 15:1–2

If a branch on a vine is left alone, it gets thicker. But as it produces more wood, it actually becomes heavier and less pro- ductive. It may look strong and healthy, but it is using more and more of the vine simply to support itself. It produces fewer and fewer grapes. It becomes unfruitful. If it continues to grow, it increases in size, but it also gets weaker and less healthy. It gets to the point that it can no longer hold the fruit it was sup- posed to bear.

But a branch cannot prune itself. It needs the gardener to cut it back, to remove all the excess wood until very little of the branches are there, and they are cut close to the vine.

Only in that weak and vulnerable pruned state, dependent on the vine, can the branches get strong and healthy enough to be fruitful again in the future.

We need to learn to identify and accept (by using the Circle[22]) when it is pruning time for us. Our modern-day definition of success (i.e., fruitfulness) has to do with growing and more growing, then bearing fruit, bearing more fruit, and growing some more. We want to go from success to even more success.

Pruning looks unproductive and often can feel like failure. If we are being successful in life, shouldn't we just work harder to maintain that success? If we have setbacks, we blame ourselves for not working hard enough. Shouldn't we use all our determination and energy to keep things going, to keep things growing? We may think so, but this is not the pattern that Jesus gives us. When a branch is *not* fruitful, it needs to be pruned back to become healthy. When a branch is fruitful, it still needs to be pruned back in order to stay healthy.

> WHEN A BRANCH IS FRUITFUL, IT STILL NEEDS TO BE PRUNED BACK IN ORDER TO STAY HEALTHY.

---

22. Information on the Circle can be found in my book *Choosing to Learn from Life*

But the reality is that although pruning is incredibly important for our wellbeing, it's not fun. In fact we dread the thought of going through it.

Let my wife Sally share an example of pruning from her life experience,

> When I was in college in Sheffield, I lived in a house with other Christian girls and was part of a large Christian community. When Mike and I got married, I joined him in Hackney. I had grown up in the suburbs; our inner-city apartment in "Devil's Island" did not exactly fulfill my dreams. Our time in Hackney was definitely one of personal pruning for me.
>
> We were serving in a very small church. We had no money, no car, no phone, and all my friends were in another part of the country. I worked from 9:00 a.m. to 5:00 p.m. at a real estate office, while Mike worked from 4:00 p.m. to 1:00 a.m. as a youth worker. We only saw each other at lunchtime. I used to cry every single day and tell him that I loved him and loved being married to him, but hated where we were living!
>
> Our time in Hackney forced me to come to grips with whether or not I truly believed that Jesus would meet all my needs. I was pruned back and all I could do was depend on the vine. I wasn't sure if I could cope with being a missionary, whether I could handle the pressures of where we were living. The valuable lessons I learned during that one year gave me a solid foundation for the next twenty. Everything except the basics of my faith was stripped away. I learned that nothing else mat- tered apart from my day-to-day walk with Jesus and my relationship with Mike. I realized that my gifts, my looks, even my heart's desires were irrelevant at that point. I needed to invest in my walk with Jesus or I wouldn't make it, nor would my marriage.
>
> —Sally

OUCH!

Sometimes when our lives are being pruned, it looks like everything is going wrong! It seems like God is working against us. It seems as though no matter what we try to do, it doesn't succeed. But isn't that the picture? Aren't you the branch and Jesus the vine? Aren't we expected to abide?

God your Father is the gardener, and he's going to cut your branches off just as soon as you bear fruit. But he is not doing it because he is mean; he is not doing it because he doesn't love you. He is doing it because he wants you to be even more fruitful, more successful in your family life, in your relationships at work and at church. But we are not going to achieve fruitfulness by living the dream and just going for it with all the energy we have. What we need to do is to get with the program and under- stand that God is not against us, he is for us—but there is a *rhythm* to life.

> GOD IS NOT AGAINST US, HE IS FOR US— BUT THERE *IS* A RHYTHM TO LIFE.

Take a look at the areas of your life where you are fruitful. Perhaps you have seen some great things happen at work. Productivity has increased, and your team is working well together. How do you maintain that success? It's tempting to think that you just need to keep going at the same pace, work- ing harder and harder.

Your kids have been doing great in school recently; they are even getting along with each other. How can you maintain the contentment in your family? Try harder, push for more, do even more stuff together?

What we really need to do is surrender ourselves to the pruning shears. Instead of even more activity, it's time to cut back and rely on the vine again.

Perhaps you were fruitful once, but not now. Things were going great, but it all seems to have dried up. Your work team used to be really effective, you used to get along great with the kids, you and your spouse used to talk. You used to love being part of the church community and you were deeply involved. Now all your stories of fruitfulness are in the past. Instead of grapes, you have raisins on your branches. Or worse yet, you feel you have to keep up the appearance that everything is going great, so you're faking it. Your branch is full of plastic grapes, so it looks like your family is doing well. From the outside, no one can judge how successful or how fruitful you really are in life. It's hidden behind a plastic smile.

It's time to be pruned, so that you can get close to Jesus again.

Jesus is saying to us, "I want to spend time with you and give you all I have. I want all that I am to flow through you so that you can be fruitful. I want you to have real success, to have the kind of fruit that lasts: families that are healed and whole, work colleagues whose lives are transformed forever through your witness, marriages that go the distance. But the way you do it is to get close to me. Abide with me; let my words feed you. I want your company."

Abiding

Growing

Bearing Fruit

Pruning

Do you see this rhythm in your life? Are you open to the idea of making some cuts in your busy schedule or freely accepting that the lull in a certain area of your life is not a call to busy yourself, but a call to abide in the Lord? Maybe you're not entirely convinced. The rhythm of life is very much a biblical concept, so let's head directly to Scripture to make the point quite clear.

CHAPTER 4

IN HIS IMAGE

Y ou look at the calendar in the office and realize that it's two weeks until you take your vacation. You are working as hard as you can so that you can take a well-deserved break. However, a lot is going on at work right now. You don't want to get caught off guard when you get back. Maybe if you just took a bit of work on vacation with you....

You're eating dinner with your family, and the kids are talk- ing about their day. Your mind keeps drifting back to the events of the office, the deadline you have to meet....

You're just about to go to bed and you decide to check your e-mail. A red flag! Something is urgent. You can't decide whether to open it or leave it until morning. It really could be urgent. It will probably only take five minutes to answer and you won't be able to sleep not knowing what it is....

It's date night and it seems like ages since you and your spouse had the chance to talk, really talk. But all you seem to talk about is work.

Do you regularly work seven days a week? Have you ever canceled a vacation because you had too much work to do? Or taken work with you? Do you have so much vacation time com- ing that soon you'll reach the company limit? Or have you broken a promise to your child to be at the big game because you felt like you couldn't get away from the office?

Have you ever not seen your kids for two days straight because you leave early for work and go straight to meetings at church in the evenings? Or do you only see your kids awake on the weekends because your commute is so long you have to leave the house before they get up in the morning, and don't return until after they've gone to bed?

Do you find at the end of a vacation, when you're finally beginning to unwind and reconnect with your family, it's time to go back to work? This wasn't exactly how you planned it, but maybe it just seems to work out like that more often than not. I'm betting these scenarios have a familiar ring to you.

And we haven't even begun to look at all the activities that our children are involved in and the amount of time and effort it takes to get them there. One has a piano lesson at the same time another has a soccer game. Then there's the work you have to do around the home—the cleaning, the repairs, and the gen- eral upkeep. Not to mention all the things you do at church. The children's ministry needs volunteers, or the service team needs ushers. And there are meetings and more meetings. A friend calls hoping to meet you for lunch to talk about a tough time. You want to be there for your friend, but so many other pressures call. How about a quick coffee instead?

It's all important stuff—work, the kids, church, friends—but how can we possibly fit it all in?

When we take a long look at our lives, plans for the abiding and fruitfulness of John 15 seem like a fantasy. It sounds like a great idea for Christians in full-time ministry. But does it work or people who live in the real world with the combined pres- sures of secular work, family, and church?

And suppose you are raising kids alone and working. What does the Semi-Circle and the rhythm of life look like then? What does it take for ordinary, everyday people to live effective, fruitful lives?

IN THE BEGINNING

Let's just do a bit of biblical detective work on this word "fruitful" so we can understand more fully what it means for everyday life. It's a common enough word in the Bible. And we will see the "rhythm of life" that Jesus described in John 15 linked to fruitfulness elsewhere in the Bible.

If we're looking for its source in Scripture, we'll find it in Genesis 1, the very first chapter in the Bible.

> Then God said, "Let us make man in our image, in our likeness, and let them rule over the fish of the sea and the birds of the air, over the livestock, over all the earth, and over all the creatures that move along the ground." So God created man in his own image, in the image of God he created him; male and female he created them. God blessed them and said to them, "Be fruitful and increase in number; fill the earth and subdue it. Rule over the fish of the sea and the birds of the air and over every living creature that moves on the ground."
>
> —Genesis 1:26–28

God said, "I'm going to make human beings in my image." We often misunderstand the word *image* because when we think of image, we think of a reflection. You know, you look in the mirror and see a reflection. Many people hang a mirror near the front door in their homes so they can check themselves just before going out. That reflection in the mirror is their own image.

But in this passage in Genesis, *image* does not mean reflection. When these words were written, there were no mirrors. The best you could do by way of reflection was to look into a pond. It's hard to fix your hair by looking into a pond.

The word *image* here is better understood as *imprint*. The Genesis story continues by saying that God formed humanity out of clay. The true picture is that God fashioned us in such a way that he left his handprint, or *imprint*, on what he made. God's intention is that the imprint is always filled with the hand that made it, so we're never further than an arm's length away from our Creator. God's plan for our lives is that his hand is always on us, filling the imprint that he left when he created us. It's a comforting thought.

> GOD'S PLAN FOR OUR LIVES IS THAT HIS HAND IS ALWAYS ON US, FILLING THE IMPRINT THAT HE LEFT WHEN HE CREATED US.

The story continues in Genesis 3. Adam and Eve strayed from God, and so they drew away and hid from the hand that made them. When God's hand is not in the imprint, our lives feel empty. Something essential is missing. In Jesus we hear the call to come back to a Father who will lay his hand on us again. He will fill the empty void with his presence.

MADE TO BE FRUITFUL

The first thing God said to Adam ; and Eve was, "Be fruitful."

He called them to a destiny, to be the overseers of all that he had made. In being overseers, they were to be fruitful. But fruitfulness was not just about hav- ing babies. It was also about being productive. Adam and Eve were left with God's handprint of creativity and productivity in their design.

> WORK IS A BLESSING OF GOD AND NOT A CURSE OF THE FALL, BECAUSE GOD WORKED IN MAKING CREATION.

Humanity has a call to produce something, and of course that would be consistent with bearing the image of God, because God had just produced the cosmos. And he is calling upon us to be coworkers with him to continue the process of creation, the process of creatures taking the stuff of the world and mak- ing something.

Now, how were Adam and Eve to be productive? What would be the means by which they would produce things? Genesis 2:15 tells us: "The LORD God took the man and put him in the Garden of Eden to work it and take care of it."

The context of human productivity is work. Human beings are supposed to work, and out of work we are supposed to be fruitful. Work is a blessing of God and not a curse of the fall, because God worked in making creation. When we work, we see the imprint of the Creator on our lives.

Let's reflect further on this. Work—being productive with our lives— is a blessing. It's OK to love working; it is how you are designed! If that work is taken away from us, we feel less than human.

This is why unemployment can be such a struggle for us. We feel as if we've fallen from what we are called to be. The focus of our productivity and fruitfulness has been taken away. We are no longer living in the way that we were created by God to live.

> We spent our early married life in an inner-city area of Bristol, England, where unemployment was always high. Our church discovered a great way of responding to the needs of our commu- nity. They got everybody involved, so although many people were unemployed, few people were short of "work." There was a lot of social outreach and activity. People were given the opportunity to live productive and fruitful lives. While we weren't knowingly applying the Semi-Circle principles to our lives then, the experience taught us how we can encourage those who are unemployed to serve so that they too can develop patterns of work and rest.
>
> —Mark and Penny

This also explains why people often struggle with retirement; years of making productive contributions to society through work suddenly come to an end. Sorry to say, but I doubt that there's any real argument from Scripture for retire- ment. Productive activity is the call of humanity. And if we just default to nothing but rest and relaxation, we're less than human. All the golf, fishing, and television in the world cannot replace a productive life! Work should always be a part of our lives. Maybe we are not always supposed to be profitably employed to do certain things. But we are always supposed to be doing intentional activity that we would normally call work.

> We live in an area in which there are a number of retired people. One of the questions we often ask is, "What do they do?" Where we live there seems to be a retirement culture of "hanging up your boots"—rest, not work. There is a limit to how many times you can wash the car or tidy the garden. People may not be able to be as active in their later years, but surely the rest/work pattern continues.

Sadly, on a number of occasions in parish life, Mark has presided at the funerals of people who died not long after they retired. Their widowed spouse will often say, "It seems so unfair that he worked so hard all his life and was just waiting to rest and enjoy life in retirement."

—Mark and Penny

And here's another thought that may be unpopular. When we look at this passage in Genesis and the parables of Jesus, we see that there is going to be work in heaven. We will not be sitting on the clouds in white gowns playing harps. (I'm sure at least some of us are relieved to discover that.) Work was an integral part of God's creation *before* the fall—it is part of what it is to be human. Even though our humanity will be fully redeemed and we'll be part of a new creation, the new creation has a connection to the old creation. In other words, the new creation is gathering up what was lost of the old creation and making it new—including work.

Then the man and his wife heard the sound of the LORD God as he was walking in the garden in the cool of the day, and they hid from the LORD God among the trees of the garden. But the LORD God called to the man, "Where are you?"

—Genesis 3:8–9

In the cool of the day, God walked through the garden seeking the company of Adam and Eve, the crown of his cre- ation. The verses suggest that this was a regular pattern where Adam and Eve reconnected with their Father; it was part of their normal existence.

But on this particular evening, Adam and Eve didn't show up. By disobeying, they had chosen to step out of the reach of the Father's hand and live without his influence. They knew what God had told them about life in the garden, but decided to choose differently. They had sinned and they knew it, so they hid.

After the fall, work changed. The fulfilling productivity of Genesis 2 was tainted. Now Adam and Eve sweated in the heat from backbreaking labor. Work itself was not a curse, but sweated labor was. It still is. Exploitative labor in sweatshops is not part of God's blessing. Working for small amounts of pay for long hours in subhuman conditions is not part of God's blessing. But fruitful productivity is.

Think about your work life. Does it feel like fruitful productivity or sweated labor?

DESIGNED TO WORK FROM REST

Right about now you are thinking, *Well, if work is a blessing from God, what's the point of this Semi-Circle? Surely we make the most of God's blessings when we work as hard as we can. Work is part of our worship to God; surely he deserves all the energy, time, and commitment? If work is from God, is there really such a thing as too much?*

But the opening chapters of Genesis tell us something else important about the way we were designed.

In the story of creation, Adam and Eve were created on the sixth day. God placed them in the garden and gave them instructions for caring for the animals and the plants around them. He told them to be fruitful.

So what happened on the following day?

Thus the heavens and the earth were com- pleted in all their vast array. By the seventh day God had finished the work he had been doing; so on the seventh day he rested from all his work.

—Genesis 2:1–2

Given that God created human beings to be in permanent contact with him, and because he's made them with the imprint that is supposed to be filled with his hand, it's inconceivable to me that on the day God rested, human beings worked.

Just think about it for a minute. If we want to understand how everyday people can live effective, fruitful lives, then we need to understand how we started, don't we? We need to know how God designed us to function. He made us on the sixth day, and after a busy day of being created, we spent the next day resting. We're made for work. We're made for fruitfulness. We're made for productive activity. But our very first full day of experience was *rest*.

Human beings are designed to work. But they're designed to work from a place of rest. Not to crash into rest from too much work. Not to crash into the weekend or vacation, tense and unable to relax. Not to crash from exhaustion. We should begin our work from a state of rest, not finally rest from too much work. God rested from his work. He can do that, he's God. But we work from rest.

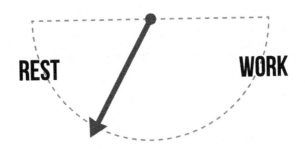

So here is the fundamental revelation that Jesus draws upon in John 15. We are made to work, but we are designed to work from rest, not rest from work. That's not some clever play on words; it's a fundamental revelation of God's creation in Scripture.

This is how we were designed to live.

PERFECT MADNESS

So often we get it the wrong way around. We know that we are supposed to be productive, but we build our identity on our activities. Instead of being human beings, we become human doings!

> INSTEAD OF BEING HUMAN BEINGS, WE BECOME HUMAN DOINGS!

We are not designed to do that. If you keep running a car in first gear, it will break down. If you keep running a car in reverse, you'll crash into others as well as break down.

What happens when we ignore the way we have been designed? We get the world we live in today. It's a world almost addictive in its vibrancy and pioneering, entrepreneurial youthfulness. It's a world always reaching for the next achievement: academically, professionally, economically, even personally. But it's also a world that is mad and getting sicker and sicker by the day. It is a world suffering all kinds of individual and collective maladies created by stress and overwork.

In an extract from her book Perfect Madness, adapted for Newsweek magazine, Judith Warner writes of the pressure many mothers face as they juggle work and family life, attempting perfection in both areas. She concludes with:

And I hope that somehow we will all find a way to stop. Because we are not doing ourselves any good. We are not doing our children—particularly our daughters—any good. We're not doing our marriages any good. And we're doing nothing at all for society.

We're simply beating ourselves black and blue. So let's take a breather. Throw out the schedules, turn off the cell phone, cancel the tutors (fire the OT!). Let's spend some real quality time with our families, just talking, hanging out, and not doing anything for once. And let ourselves be.[23]

Let's be honest. We Christians are no different! We often justify this behavior by saying we are doing it for God.

As I began to see this concept of working from rest, I wondered why I managed to read the first two chapters of the Bible countless times and had never seen it. Maybe it was just because I was a pastor, designed to strive. But when you read the Bible over and over again, you find hidden depths. It's truly exciting. When I finally did see it, another thought began to emerge in my mind. If this is the way that God made the world, we should see evidence of this outside of Scripture. We should see evidence of this out there in the "real world"—the living, breathing world.[24]

If people function without rest, they don't do well. That's just fact, proven over and over. Certain countries have experimented with having no days of rest. During World War II, Russia tried this and productivity plummeted. Other countries, such as France, have tried it. Their productivity plummeted. Fruitfulness was cut short because people were not able to be people. And people need to rest. Rest is not a particularly live issue in the minds of industrialized nations, but

23. Judith Warner, "Mommy Madness," *Newsweek*, February 21, 2005.
24. I'll have another story for you in chapter 9.

stress certainly is. So I'm not the only one ringing these alarm bells, but I may be the only one delivering this solution to you.

If you are like me, a kairos moment is opening up. Remember,

a kairos moment is an event in your life—big or small, positive or negative—that sparks an inner desire to make some sort of change in your life. That change occurs by walking through the learning circle and will result in making you a stronger disciple of Jesus.

So right now you are probably beginning to think, *OK, stop right now! I don't want to hear any more of this; I want to ignore this part!*

Do you rest from work, or work from rest?

The overwhelming question that comes up when we start to look at this stuff is how? How do we begin to work from rest when we know no other way of doing things and everyone else is playing by the same insane set of standards? How do you make this work? Whatever you do, don't stop now. Keep reading.

CHAPTER 5

LEARN FROM JESUS

The car is gassed up. You've got a bag of snacks to sustain you and a suitcase in the backseat. You're ready for your trip. At the last minute you stick a map in the pocket of the driver's door. It's an old map, but you don't expect to need it anyway. You're headed somewhere you've been many times. You can remember traveling with your family often to Aunt Ellen's as you were growing up—nearly every summer and for many Thanksgivings as well.

You hit the highway, confident that you know what you're doing. A few hours down the road, you reminisce about your last visit with Aunt Ellen and your cousins: the little shop down the street where you went to buy Dr. Pepper; the drugstore on Front Street where Aunt Ellen took you for snow cones; the pasture where you and your cousins sat on the fence and imagined the horses were yours. It's been ten years since you last made this trip, and along the way things are starting to look different. At one intersection where there used to be a gas station and a mom-and-pop grocery store, you see a strip mall full of chain stores. You're sure this road used to be two lanes and now it's four. The names of the streets aren't even right.

At another intersection you finally admit to yourself that you're not sure which way to turn. Waiting while the light is red, you scan the landscape. Pastures have turned into subdivisions and meadows into tidy city parks. The topography is flat, the sun is high in the sky, and everything around you is nothing like you remember. You have no idea which way is north, much less where Aunt Ellen's house is.

Up ahead of you is a Walmart, of all things. Where did that come from? When the light turns green, you decide Walmart is a good thing and pull in the parking lot to look at your map. But you didn't expect to need the map, remember? It's so old that it's not really much use. You've got to figure out what town you're in.

You're lost.

> This is what the LORD says:
> "Stand at the crossroads and look;
> ask for the ancient paths,
> ask where the good way is, and walk in it,
> and you will find rest for your souls."
>
> —Jeremiah 6:16

You may feel that once upon a time, taking a day off or a vacation was straightforward. But now it seems impossible. Sometimes it's hard to get a sense of direction for working out a rhythm for our lives. You might think, *How did I get here?* More importantly, how do you get to where you want to be? We look for signposts that will point the way, but they are confusing. They only raise more questions. *What about my boss? What about my family? How will we do financially? Will my kids miss out on opportunities? What will my church leaders think?*

When the map is out of date and the signposts have changed, the only thing you can be sure of is a compass. No matter what the landscape looks like, directions never change, and you can be sure that a compass will put you on the right track. They may not appear as sophisticated or complex as using a map or GPS, but compasses have been around for centuries. They are ancient, but they are also reliable. It was simpler once, but the landscape of our lives—and our society—has changed. We have dual-career households. We have kids who move from one structured activity to another rather than riding their bikes around the neighborhood, which is really no longer safe to do in most cases. We have second mortgages and an array of credit cards that make anything possible. We have to fight competition to hang onto our jobs as businesses outsource or technology replaces workers. We have electronic gizmos coming out our ears even though most of us don't know what to do with them. We have come up with all kinds of sophisticated and complicated devices to help us on the journey through life. But the truth is, they aren't really getting us anywhere.

> WHEN THE MAP IS OUT OF DATE AND THE SIGNPOSTS HAVE CHANGED, THE ONLY THING YOU CAN BE SURE OF IS A COMPASS.

We are low on gas, tired, and increasingly frustrated. We are at a crossroads. We need to find the ancient path. We need to find the simple way to get through life. We need something that remains the same yesterday, today, and forever. **We need a compass, and our compass is Jesus.**

> Come to me, all you who are weary and burdened, and I will give you rest. Take my yoke upon you and learn from me, for I am gentle and humble in heart, and you will find rest for your souls. For my yoke is easy and my burden is light.
>
> —Matthew 11:28–30

Everything that Jesus said and did points the way to how we are supposed to live. And that's not just about our salvation and what to think about the world. We are his disciples, meaning we are lifelong learners. We study his life for more than information about him. We want to be like him, to imitate him, to live how he lived. His life is the pattern we need to follow for our journey.

If all the things we have said about the rhythm of life are true, then we should see it in Jesus' life. He knew the pressures of a busy schedule. Many people in his life constantly made demands on his time. He had an important job to do, and limited time in which to get it done. How did he do it?

ON THE MOVE

When Mark tells the story of Jesus, we see a passionate life on the move. Everything's incredible or astonishing or amazing or "at once." That's the way that Mark wrote the story. It's almost as if he wrote a comic book—the Marvel version of the life of Jesus. Imagine the speech bubbles: "Wow!" and "Whoa!" and "Zowie!"

> At that time Jesus came from Nazareth in Galilee and was baptized by John in the Jordan. As Jesus was coming up out of the water, he saw heaven being torn open and the Spirit descending on him like a dove. And a voice came from heaven: "You are my Son, whom I love; with you I am well pleased."
>
> At once the Spirit sent him out into the desert, and he was in the desert forty days, being tempted by Satan. He was with the wild animals, and angels attended him.
>
> —Mark 1:9–13

What an amazing experience for Jesus. He comes out of the water, the sky is torn apart, and we get a glimpse beyond the physical realm into the spiritual realm. A dove, the symbol of the Holy Spirit, descends upon him. Out of that open portal from heaven the voice of God says, "You are my Son."

You would think the next thing would be, "Let's get on with it, then." Instead, the Holy Spirit immediately takes Jesus from the Jordan and directs him into the wilderness where he waits on God for forty days. Mark tells us that, not surprisingly, at the end of those forty days Jesus is hungry. And at that point the Devil tempts him.

> EVEN AFTER ALL
> THE WAITING,
> JESUS' MINISTRY
> STARTS WITH
> RETREAT.

So, what does this tell us? Jesus lives by the same principles of abiding and fruitfulness that we have seen throughout the Bible. We've already seen it in Adam and Eve, and we know it's true of the disciples. It was also the story of the apostle Paul, who was converted and went immediately into a time of learning.

We begin from the place of retreat. We begin "with God" before we go "from God." Jesus has been hidden pretty much the first thirty years of his life. He is about to begin the great season of ministry in his life. Even after all the waiting, his ministry starts with retreat.

IN STEP WITH LIFE

The pattern of beginning with retreat is not just a seasonal thing; it's a daily thing. We see this rhythm further on in the same chapter of Mark.

First, Jesus got his team together. He gathered the guys and called
them fishers of men. No one knew quite what that meant yet,
but they followed him anyway. On the first day of his ministry in
Capernaum, Jesus went into the synagogue. The people were amazed
by his teaching. Then someone at the back of the room started
screaming, so Jesus cast out a demon. This was not your average day
at the synagogue. People woke up and paid attention. The next stop
was Peter's house, where his mother-in-law was sick. Apparently, in
this group of men there was nobody to cook, so when Jesus healed
her, she got up and started cooking for them. It wasn't long before
the word got out about the incredible things this guy was up to. That
evening, the entire city came to the door, wanting to meet Jesus.

With such a crowd gathered around, it is no wonder a paralyzed
man couldn't get in without being lowered through the roof. Jesus
had healed the sick and cast out demons. That night, people camped
out all around Peter's house, getting some sleep before tomorrow's
adventures.

But Jesus had other plans.

> Very early in the morning, while it was still dark,
> Jesus got up, left the house and went off to a solitary
> place, where he prayed. Simon and his companions
> went to look for him, and when they found him, they
> exclaimed: "Everyone is looking for you!"

> Jesus replied, "Let us go somewhere else— to the nearby
> villages—so I can preach there also. That is why I have
> come." So he traveled throughout Galilee, preaching in
> their synagogues and driving out demons.

> —Mark 1:35–39

So what did Jesus do? He spent one day in ministry, and then he disappeared. We can imagine the conversation the next day among the disciples.

Peter: Where's Jesus? I can't find him anywhere! There's a line of people outside and they say they won't go until they've met him!

Andrew: I dunno.

Peter: What do you mean you don't know? Did you see him leave?

Andrew: Nope.

Peter: John, James, did you see where he went?

John: Nope.

James: Not a word to me.

Peter: You just let him get away? He's disappeared. We have got to find him before these people knock the door down!

They searched the city looking for Jesus, asking everyone, but there was no sign of him. Then someone said, "There was a guy walking into the hills very early this morning. Don't know if it was him, though."

It was the only lead they had. They went up to the hills and eventually found Jesus. He was praying.

The disciples coughed loudly. They didn't want to be rude, but a lot of people were waiting down in the city. They had been waiting a while now. Jesus turned to them and said, "Hello."

"Jesus," Peter said, "what are you doing? Revival is taking place down there in Capernaum. Don't you know we should be raising the tent,

> IT'S SIMPLE.
>
> BUT WE STILL
>
> DON'T GET IT.
>
> WE STILL KEEP
>
> TRYING TO PUMP
>
> UP THE FRUIT
>
> PRODUCTION
>
> WITHOUT ANY
>
> ABIDING TIME.

starting the tape ministry, and having daily meetings both morning and evening? This is what everybody has been waiting for!"

Jesus just smiled and replied, "Let's go somewhere else."

The disciples stared at him in disbelief. And we would have done exactly the same thing. Yet Luke tells us that Jesus retreated like this on a regular basis. "But Jesus often withdrew to lonely places and prayed" (Luke 5:16). His regular pattern, his basic discipline, was retreat and then adventure, rest and then work.

In other words, the pattern established in the early days of Jesus' ministry—beginning with rest and followed by retreat to be with God—continued through the rest of his ministry. If we are to be disciples learning how to *live* like Jesus, why is that pattern not in our lives both individually and collectively? There has to be a reason for it, and I think we really need to ask— and answer—that question.

Jesus said unless you abide in me, you cannot bear fruit. Unless you retreat with me, you can't be fruitful and effective in life. Unless you return to me, you can't be productive.

It's simple. But we still don't get it. We still keep trying to pump up the fruit production without any abiding time.

LEARN LIKE THE DISCIPLES

Mark shows us that Jesus taught this pattern of life to his disciples, too.

> Calling the Twelve to him, he sent them out two by two
> and gave them authority over evil spirits.
>
> —Mark 6:7

Up until this point, Jesus had been doing most of the ministry. But the disciples were an example of how fruitful Jesus was, for they multiplied his ministry throughout Galilee. By sending them out on a mission in six different teams, Jesus was finally giving the disciples a piece of the action. And they had such a profound effect on the wider community that thousands followed them back to Capernaum.

This drew even more people, which provided an even greater opportunity to bear fruit. You would think with all this activity going on that Jesus would say, "Guys, it's time to have a revival meeting every day." But Jesus responded to the situation with a call to rest.

> Then, because so many people were coming and going
> that they did not even have a chance to eat, he said to
> them, "Come with me by yourselves to a quiet place
> and get some rest."
>
> —Mark 6:31

Why did he do that? Why did Jesus respond in the exact opposite way from how we've been conditioned to respond?

Well, the problem with Jesus is that he did what God wanted him to do rather than what his human nature told him was the obvious thing to do. He said, "Guys, this is great. But it's never going to be sustainable unless you get into the pattern that God has for you. Let's get away and rest."

Well, they got into the boat, and you know the story. The people guessed where they were going and ran on ahead of them. When Jesus and the disciples arrived, five thousand families were there waiting for them.

Five thousand families! Just imagine how many people were there. We twenty-first-century Westerners think, "Wow, it must have been twenty thousand people!" People in other parts of the world laugh at us. It's amusing that we assume families only have two children. In many cultures, families have *lots* of children. The Bible just says that five thousand heads-of-household were there. Who knows how many thousands of people were there. They covered the whole hillside.

So Jesus taught them, and at the end of the day he fed them. Then Jesus turned to the guys and said, "Okay, I'm going to get rid of the crowd now. You go out through the back exit. Take the lake and head for Bethsaida. I'll dismiss them. You go."

He sent the crowd away. Then he went up a mountain to pray. The disciples probably hadn't thought about how Jesus was going to get to them. After all, they had the boat. That night they discovered Jesus could walk on water.

Jesus created an exit strategy for himself and his disciples to get away from the busyness. Mark tells us that eventually,

> Jesus left that place and went to the vicinity of Tyre. He entered a house and did not want anyone to know it; yet he could not keep his presence secret.
>
> —Mark 7:24

Remember, Mark's gospel is packed with the "wow" factor, the "whoa, you'll never believe this!" The significance in this verse is that Jesus left the land of Israel to go and get some rest. He went to the vicinity of Tyre, even though that's outside the land of his people. He'd come specifically to reach out to the people of Israel; but to get his disciples away from the busyness, he took them to another country.

ASK FOR THE ANCIENT PATHS

> This is what the LORD says:
> "Stand at the crossroads and look;
> ask for the ancient paths,
> ask where the good way is, and walk in it,
> and you will find rest for your souls."
>
> —Jeremiah 6:16

There's one more line to this verse: "But you said, 'We will not walk in it.'"

How stubborn we are sometimes, refusing the way that God has made clear to us.

What will you use to navigate your way through a hectic life? What journey will you take to live a fruitful, effective life? Will you use a map outlining your goals, your ambitions, and your game plans? Or sophisticated, complex tools that are supposed to guide your way? Maybe you hope your own sense of direction, your inner determination and drive will get you there.

Or will you try God's perfect plan for us—the old-fashioned, simple compass—instead?

The poet Robert Frost wrote:

> I shall be telling this with a sigh
> Somewhere ages and ages hence:
> Two roads diverged in a wood, and I—
> I took the one less traveled by,
> And that has made all the difference.
>
> —The Road Not Taken

Jesus still calls his disciples to walk along a path that often goes in the opposite direction to the world around us. Do you have the courage to walk in it?

CHAPTER 6

REST UP TO WORK

Y̲ou were so organized last night. You made a list of the tasks you need to accomplish today so that you can relax this weekend, spend some time with the kids, putter in the woodshop or the garden, and maybe even take in a movie. The morning starts out with determination and optimism.

By 3:30 in the afternoon, the picture has turned inside out. An emergency meeting at work has consumed your morning and added more urgent tasks to your list. You didn't even have time to eat your lunch, much less get to the bank, the drugstore, and the library on your lunch break. The school called to say your son is running a fever. You go and pick him up, but you have to go back to work. Your boss wants that report first thing in the morning so he doesn't get in hot water with the vice president. It's so hard to ask for help, and it takes four phone calls to find someone who can help care for your son, plus you have to drive halfway across town to get him there. You'll never make it to the dry cleaners before they close. The worship ministry team is expecting you for a 7:00 rehearsal. You're in charge, so you can't skip.

You feel the weight on your shoulders. For too many of us, this is a typical day. And tomorrow will be another just like it. The list of "must do" tasks for the day is impossibly long under the best of circumstances. Under the tyranny of the urgent, just the mention of rest makes us feel worse, because there is no time to fit it in.

THE BIG PICTURE

Step back. Look at the bigger picture of your life. In the Breen household, we don't wait until we are tired before we plan a vacation. We look at the whole year in advance.

We look at the pattern of our children's school year. We look at the calendar and take note of weddings, anniversaries, births, and other significant events. We look at our work schedules. At the start of the year, we schedule our time off. This is an important principle for every stage of life—single, married, a young family, or retired.

> Sometimes its important to look at the whole year and work out where the stresses are going to be well in advance. If you have major life events happening like exams, retirement, or babies being born it's a good idea to plan a time of rest before those events happen.
>
> It's possible sometimes to take a vacation at another time of the year than usual so that you can accommodate these expected and known life events. It also means you can get help when you know you might need it from your extended family (*Oikos*).
>
> I know this is not always possible. When our newest granddaughter was born 5 weeks early our plans had to change, However where possible its good to plan ahead a year at a time.
>
> -Sally

Take your calendar and look at the year as a whole. There are many things that you cannot predict or prepare for. You may not know when a project at work will be particularly demanding. You cannot plan when your child may go through a tough time at school. You can't plan for an illness or an accident. But you can be proactive and schedule vacation interludes throughout the year so that you have a foundation of working from a place of rest when these things happen. Hold to these vacation commitments. This will help you to be fruitful and effective in the unexpected situations that zap so much strength.

> IT'S NOT JUST THE YEAR THAT NEEDS A SENSE OF RHYTHM. EVERY LEVEL OF OUR LIVES BENEFITS FROM THE PRINCIPLE OF WORKING FROM REST.

ANTICIPATE PRESSURE POINTS

It's not just the year that needs a sense of rhythm. Every level of our lives benefits from the principle of working from rest.

MONTHLY. When we take time to look at monthly patterns, we see the kinds of pressure points that creep up on us because they do not take place quite as regularly. Sit down and look at your schedule for the upcoming month. The car needs servicing. There is a parent/teacher conference at the end of the month. You've been invited out for a meal next week. It's Mother's Day in three weeks. It's also good to look at things like birthdays, anniversaries, children's sports tournaments, and people coming to visit. Does it work for your family life if you have people stay with you for a week during a really demanding month at work? Or when the children have exams?

When you look at your month, you might also include seasonal household chores. It's time to spray the yard for weeds, clean out the garage, that sort of thing. Depending on your personality and preference, these tasks could be a chance to recreate and relax—or a nightmare you want to avoid.

WEEKLY. To find a weekly rhythm, look at the week as a whole. As you do this, include every member of your household, visitors included. This makes it easier to see the points of stress, but also the points of opportunity. When we see the whole week, we realize we can take Tuesday off, or that Thursday might be particularly full. You would then know that you should prioritize time with family and friends, making sure to get in a family dinner on Wednesday.

Another significant part of a weekly rhythm is taking a day off; we'll look at that more in another chapter.

> When I look at our family schedule, I use a whiteboard in the kitchen. I write down the major events of the week for each family member. Sam may be playing lacrosse on Wednesday night; Mike needs to get the car serviced on Friday morning.
>
> Mealtimes are key. It's helpful to have a plan of what we're going to eat at every mealtime so that the stress is taken out of having to think about it. It helps make the meals a focus point in our day. We woke our children up so they could eat breakfast together, even as teenagers! Mealtimes give us the chance to talk and be together as a family. However, this time is not exclusive; friends often join us for meals.
>
> When the children were younger, if Mike couldn't get away from the office but did have an hour's break, we would take a picnic down to his office and hang out there together. Sometimes we would meet at a fast food restaurant.
>
> —Sally

DAILY. Broken down even further, our days can have a sense of rhythm, of rest and work. But we need to plan a rhythm that works for the stage of life we are in. To help us in this, we can divide the day into four segments:

> Breakfast to Lunch.
> Lunch to 4:00 p.m.
> 4:00 to 7:00 p.m.
> 7:00 p.m. to Bedtime.

Your goal should be to take off one portion of the day for rest. When we say "off," we don't necessarily mean ignoring the children for a time of solitude. That portion of the day can be time recreating with children. Just make it a break from the normal pressures, or even better, include some time of intentional abiding in God.

> Over the years, I have learned to be more aware of everyone's stress points within a day. My lowest point in the day is 4:00 in the afternoon. I am low in energy, interest, and focus. But it was also the time when the children came home from school! I had to plan ahead. Whenever possible, I used the slow cooker to have the evening meal prepared by 4:00 p.m. I would make sure the children had snacks ready for them when they walked in the door. Instead of having to rush around preparing meals and snacks when I had no energy, I could sit down with a cup of tea and talk to them about their day. Life was a lot more fun for all of us that way.
>
> —Sally

Take a moment to reflect on your own daily routine. At what point in the day do you have the most energy? The least energy? Are you a morning or night person? How does that affect how you rest? How does that affect how you work? Consider each of your family members as well. You can help them combat their low energy times, or at least have an extra ounce of patience and understanding when you're aware they're in the midst of a low energy time. This has the

> WE ARE NOT ALWAYS IN CONTROL OF WHEN WE WORK, BUT WE CAN STILL LOOK AT WAYS THAT WE CAN BE PREPARED FOR PRESSURE.

potential to diffuse some stressful times in the household.

PRACTICAL PLANNING

Be practical as you plan your points of rest and work. We are all too aware of the external pressures that shape our day. We are not always in control of when we work, but we can still look at ways that we can be prepared for pressure. Where are your stress points in the day? Morning, afternoon, schooltime, evening?

> We have made a point as a family of saying good morning at the start of the day and good night at the end.
>
> Nobody drifts to bed and nobody drifts awake. It is a rhythm. We all get up together; this is what we do. We're not afraid to call the family together to start the day. Even if Mike is away, he will call or send a text message. It is part of our daily rhythm as a family.
>
> —Sally

Every family will have its own stress points in the daily routine, and of course so will each family member. It may be getting a teenager out of bed in the morning—literally. It may be working out the transportation logistics to get everyone where they have to be. It may be slogging through homework challenges with a discouraged, emotional seventh grader. You know what they are for your family. Look at the pieces of your day and brainstorm together how you can prepare for the stress points and successfully destress everyone.

> Our school mornings were becoming a nightmare. There were five of us to get up, feed, dress, and walk out of the house with all the day's necessities by 8:30 a.m. We were all

stressed. Add into that scenario a baby with extra practical needs and we were sinking. We decided to be proactive in easing the time pressure in the mornings. The night before, we'd get out all the kids' school clothes, sort out packed lunch boxes, put out breakfast, etc. When we did this, the whole morning ran more smoothly.

Now that our children are a little older, we get some individual space early in the morning before they are up. This means we, too, start the day from rest and not from frenetic activity. Our church has a "Start-the-Week Bible Study." This helps us to begin the week in the right way—focused on God. Another idea that worked in our family is that Mark started running three times a week, first thing in the morning, and feels the benefits for himself in terms of effectiveness. He has more stamina, is more alert, and feels better about the day.

We've discovered for ourselves that part of being proactive is preparation time. We had to look at how we viewed the start of the day.

Was it merely a time to survive, or a time to get ready for an effective and productive time of work? We are learning the importance of preparation as part of our rhythm of life.

—Mark and Penny

HOW DO YOU REST?

How do you get refreshed? We all do it differently. Before you begin to practice the Semi-Circle, it's important to discover how *you* rest.

Are you an extrovert or an introvert? Believe it or not, this makes a difference in how you rest and what activities you find relaxing. In general terms, extroverts think by talking. They download information by processing it with someone else. They brainstorm by thinking out loud, bouncing their ideas off another person. If you need a spur-of-the-moment speech, an extrovert is the one who will step up to the challenge. An extrovert's idea of a refreshing weekend might be a big party, rowdy games, loud music—the more people the better.

Not so for introverts. They tend to process information internally. Introverts will not be the ones to take over a meeting by talking too much. Quite the opposite. They'll sit and process what they hear, and they tend to think before they speak. If you give them a new idea, you may need to allow thinking time before expecting feedback. Creative types—painters, writers, composers—often are introverts, being their most creative when they are alone. In terms of rest, an introvert might prefer time alone, reading a good book, or renting a movie.

If you are more of an extrovert, don't be surprised if a quiet evening by yourself does not refresh you. You'll probably get bored with yourself in the first ten minutes. You'll exhaust yourself with the effort of being alone. So don't make the mistake of thinking that resting means isolating yourself. Spend time with friends. On the other hand, if you are more of an introvert, don't feel bad about thinking that you'd much rather read a book than hang out at the cookout trying to think of something clever to say. Of course you cannot avoid people forever, but you know yourself well enough to know you need to spend at least a portion of your time alone. Obviously we all need to develop a personal relationship with God, and he will refresh us regardless of personality type. But don't ignore the way God created you to be. Celebrate it.

> The whole introvert/extrovert concept was an eye opener for us. It has helped us realize that rest isn't necessarily sleeping or even sitting down! We are very different in how we rest. For Penny, the best thing is an empty house, some music, and something to cook. Mark's idea of rest is to have lots of people around to shoot the breeze and eat with!

> We try to give each other space to relax in the way that best compliments our personalities. However, as a couple we sometimes have to compromise. This is one of our weakest areas, so we are working on it.

> Our weekly pattern is to take Friday nights as a night for

us. Maybe watch TV, get takeout, see a film, have friends in for a meal. Daily, during our late afternoon slot, we try to sit down on our own after we have eaten as a family. Mark also works a lot of evenings. We try to take a slot in the daytime once a week to go out as a couple, even if it's only for coffee or a walk.

—Mark and Penny

So what do you do to relax? Make your own list. Don't choose something off of someone else's list. Physical activity may invigorate you, so get out and work in the yard. When you're finished shoveling your driveway, do the one across the street. Leisurely strolls with favorite music playing in your ears may be just the thing for you. Picking through antiques. Flea markets. Visiting historical sites. Semiprofessional baseball. Crafts or woodworking, gardening or decorating. Organizing a group outing for thirty of your closest friends. Running a 10K. Snoozing in the hammock once in a while. Taking your kids to the park. Reading through the new fiction shelf at the library. An annual mission trip. Rest is whatever makes you take a deep sigh and say, "God is good."

> REST IS WHATEVER MAKES YOU TAKE A DEEP SIGH AND SAY, "GOD IS GOOD.

ESTABLISH A PLACE OF REST

When you look at your home or your office, does it help to make you feel relaxed? Or does it add to the stress of the day?

It may seem insignificant, but it's hard to work from a place of rest in the office when you can't even see your desk. You always have that nagging feeling that underneath the pile of paper is something urgent that you were supposed to attend to. And occasionally you are right! Every time you walk past piles of books on the floor, you scold yourself for not putting those books on the shelf yet.

Then there is your home. Try to see it afresh through the eyes of a first-time visitor. How do you arrange your house for the people living in it? When you think about your home, it's no good interpreting everything just through your personality. You have to communicate and see how other members of the household relax and unwind. If you still have boxes to unpack from your move nine months ago, that may make your children feel crowded or unsettled. If you have a young adult who is a night person, and another who is more of a morning person, then the TV shouldn't be close to the morning person's bedroom. Are there rooms in your home that make you feel stressed just by entering them? Your environment truly matters in conveying a feeling of tranquility.

Over the years, we have lived in twelve different houses and owned twenty-eight cars and six motorbikes and bicycles (one of them was plastic!). Alongside raising three children and a foster daughter, we have had three dogs, eight rabbits, two hamsters, two cats, and several people share our home. In our first ten months of living in Arizona, we spent only twenty-eight days without visitors. It's been a challenging, exciting, adventurous existence so far and we don't see that changing! But we have learned with every home we've lived in, it is essential to our well-being as a family and to our ministry that our home is a safe and settled place of rest.

The practicalities of this have changed as our family has changed. As the children grew older, they could get more involved in the household chores. When we moved to Arizona, it was definitely a family affair. It was not only a fun adventure for us all, but now the whole family is involved in establishing our house as a home, a place of rest. Even though the girls are at college in England and Sam is in his teens, the home is still a place of retreat and rest.

I love my house; it's a wonderful blessing. But the utility room gets me stressed. It's tiny and I walk through it every time I enter the house from the garage. I see five people's sets of clothing waiting to be washed or put away. And they rarely wait in a tidy pile. Sometimes the easy option is simply to close the door. But it's not long before one of the family or a visitor enters the house through the utility room, and there it is for all of us to see.

On a smaller scale, I try to have certain things in place to avoid feeling stressed. The beds need to be made. I like having fresh flowers. I even like having a clean kettle! Now these are obviously my preferences, but they help make our house feel like a home to me.

—Sally

CHILDREN WORK FROM REST

Where do children fit into all of this? What should we be teaching them about rest?

> Train a child in the way he should go, and when he is old he will not turn from it.
>
> —Proverbs 22:6

Rest is not just for grown-ups; it's for children, too. We all know the importance of establishing healthy patterns in our children's lives while they are young. These healthy patterns will help them after they have left the nest. This is true of work and rest; early patterns and routines have a big impact on how children will develop their own patterns of work and rest later in life.

> EARLY PATTERNS AND ROUTINES HAVE A BIG IMPACT ON HOW CHILDREN WILL DEVELOP THEIR OWN PATTERNS OF WORK AND REST LATER IN LIFE.

But many parents have demanding jobs with long hours. For some

children this can mean being dropped off early in the morning at
before school care, going to school, then after school clubs and social
activities. In the evenings parents may keep kids up late in order to
spend time with them. Having to juggle jobs and family brings added
pressures and challenges to the pattern of working from rest. Kids get
caught in the undertow of their parents' lives. An elementary school
teacher observed that some children arrive at school worn out.

> Life today for children can be packed with a constant
> round of social activities. The current trend where we live is
> to invite all the children in your class to your birthday party.
>
> That's a lot of parties to attend! While of course these are
> all good things in themselves, the current message seems to
> be to fill your children's lives with as much as possible or they
> will miss out!
>
> While it's important to give children opportunities, we
> need to strike a balance, especially when you have several chil-
> dren. Otherwise life is a constant round of activity for both
> children and parents. We are now rearranging our weekends
> because they were in danger of being swamped with ballet,
> soccer, drama, and everything else kids can do.
>
> —Mark and Penny

In a particularly telling case, a group of kids had trouble settling
down to sleep at night and were referred to a sleep clinic. In all but
one case, the children did not have sleep disorders. Instead, what
became apparent was that the children had no rhythm of rest in
their evenings. In response, the therapists specified an order to the
children's evenings. The children were given time to unwind and rest
with books and quiet activities before bed. They slept much better.
This may seem obvious to most parents, but we live in a busy world
where children soon pick up patterns of activity. The concept of rest
needs to be learned and practiced in the home. How often do you
hear a child saying that he or she *wants* to go to bed? When children
get too busy and don't sleep as well, it affects their behavior and then
the *whole* family suffers.

Children rest in different ways according to their personalities, just as adults do. We have two extrovert children and one introvert. Understanding this concept has helped us understand how they "rest." One of our children loves to play alone in his bedroom and needs to do this. The other two need friends and family around, which often means a noisy household!

—Mark and Penny

WHAT NEXT?

There are many more applications of rest and work to explore on your own. Feel free to utilize this book by starting with the points that are most pressing for where you are in your walk right now.

Some of us know in theory that we need to apply these principles of balancing rest and work, but we need help getting started. We sometimes need community to help us bridge the gaps in our lives. Getting help and support is usually not about being able to pay for it. When Sally and I moved to Phoenix, we left behind all of our biological family—aunts, uncles, cousins, and grandparents. But we did move over with a number of friends who are our extended family. This family became even larger as we got to know people at our church. We'll look at the impact that being part of a community can have on work and rest in a later chapter.

For others, rest is not a problem. We know how to rest. The challenge is to be more productive, to make a contribution somehow. Again, the chapter that looks at community may show you how you can get more involved. What we have discovered is that different seasons of life can present us with either greater opportunities or certain restrictions. We'll look at some of those seasons beginning in chapter 11.

There may be some of you who are thinking, "I agree with every word you say, but it's not up to me. My boss, pastor, spouse, etc. calls the shots." The following chapter on Daniel contains some practical ideas on how to tackle that difficult situation. I think you'll feel at first convicted, and then encouraged by its suggestions.

Finally, for some of you, looking at the big picture and general principles helps, but you need to take things one step at a time. You need a place to start. Why not start with one day? Chapter 8 looks at taking just one day off a week—albeit the most important of all—the Sabbath. Now that you have a strong understanding of the importance of working from rest, we'll take a look at applying this principle to our hectic, twenty- first-century lives.

CHAPTER 7

"BUT YOU DON'T KNOW MY BOSS!"

A thirst for world dominance was in the blood of Nebuchadnezzar of Babylon. His father sought it and failed. But Nebuchadnezzar pressed forward, squelching Egypt, the only serious opponent on his way to supremacy. Now Nebuchadnezzar's major task was to march through the territory he had won and demand submission, city by city. Jehoiachin, king of Judah, was a rookie eighteen-year-old monarch who was no threat. The Babylonians entered Jerusalem and carried him and the rest of the royal family off to captivity with little resistance.

Nebuchadnezzar had another agenda as well: He wanted the best and the brightest of the captured people to serve in Babylon as court advisers and leaders. The best craftsmen were on his list as well. He took ten thousand of Jerusalem's most talented citizens to Babylon and left behind a plundered city, a desecrated temple, and a demoralized population with no leaders or resources to rebuild. Nebuchadnezzar had exactly what he wanted.

Once in Babylon, some of the promising young men from the Jewish nobility were selected for an intensive training program. The program was to last three years and by the end of it, the best of the best would serve as advisers in Nebuchadnezzar's royal court.

Daniel and his three friends Hananiah, Mishael, and Azariah were selected for the training program. They would learn a new language so they could speak like Babylonians. They would learn Babylonian literature so they could think like Babylonians. They would be immersed in a new way of looking at life, a new set of values. By the end of the three years of training, these young men would think, act, speak, even *be* Babylonian. Judah would be a distant memory of their youth, surpassed by the greatness of this brand new world. As if to emphasize this, Daniel and his three friends' names were changed. Hananiah, Mishael, and Azariah became Shadrach, Meshach, and Abednego. Daniel, whose name meant "God is my judge," was renamed Belteshazzar, meaning "Bel protect his life."

As part of his tempting sales pitch, Nebuchadnezzar wanted the trainees to see what an extravagant life they could have with just a bit of cooperation on their part. Although they were captives, they could eat sumptuous food from the royal menu. The finest food and wine of the empire were at their fingertips.

Not bad for a group of exiles. This wasn't at all the way they had imagined captivity on the long march from Jerusalem to Babylon. Sure, they were far from home, but they were starting to think the trade-off was worth it. Surely life would be better now than ever. This was a chance to progress, to really get somewhere in life. In Judah, even if they had reached the pinnacle of fame and power, their influence would have been over only a small, forgotten place, insignificant in the scheme of world power. But here in Babylon, they could rise to high positions in government and influence the most powerful empire in the world. Chances like this were once in a lifetime. They would have the best of everything.

There was one small problem. There's no such thing as a free lunch. And Daniel knew it. It didn't matter where he was or who was king. God ruled his life, and he followed God's guidelines. It didn't matter what language he spoke, or what he was given to read. They could try to change his name, but it wouldn't change who he really was, or whose he really was. He belonged to God and lived for him.

The food may have been great, but it went against the dietary restrictions that God had given the Israelites. Choosing to eat the food would have meant putting the Babylonian world before Daniel's relationship with God.

THE CHOICE

> But Daniel resolved not to defile himself with the royal food and wine.
>
> —Daniel 1:8

Daniel's first response was internal. He worked out what his values were, what he stood for, and how he would live his life. He could not do anything about the surroundings he lived in. He couldn't just walk out the door and hop a bus back to Jerusalem. But he could remain true to God in the way he lived his life even in a place like Babylon.

Daniel could have been defiant, refusing outright to touch the king's food. That might have cost him his life and would have achieved very little in the end. Perhaps God did have him in Babylon for a purpose. It just needed to be on God's terms.

And he asked the chief official for permission not to
defile himself this way.

—Daniel 1:8

At the end of the day the royal officials didn't want to get into trouble
with the king, so Daniel simply suggested an experiment to see what
would work best. "Why not put me to the test?" asked Daniel. "In
fact, test the four of us, Hananiah, Mishael, Azariah, and myself. Give
us a simple diet of vegetables and water for ten days. Then compare
us with the other trainees who eat the royal food. You can make your
decision based on what you see. If we're doing better than everybody
else by eating our stuff and not your stuff, then you'll just let us do
that.

DANIEL IS
A GREAT
CHARACTER
FOR TWENTY-
FIRST- CENTURY
DISCIPLES TO
RELATE TO.
HE WAS OUT
THERE IN THE
REAL WORLD, A
WORLD WITH A
DIFFERENT SET
OF VALUES AND
PRINCIPLES.

How about that?"

The officials had nothing to lose. At the
end of the test, Daniel and

his friends were in much better shape than
the other trainees, so they were allowed to
continue with their diet. God equipped
them with all the skills and gifts they
needed. At the end of the three years, they
went before the king. Nebuchadnezzar
saw that the four young men were way
ahead of the rest. When they entered the
king's service, he found that their advice
and insights were far better than all the
magicians and enchanters in his kingdom.
Daniel and his friends rose to positions of
great influence in the years to come.

DANIEL IN THE TWENTY-FIRST CENTURY

Daniel is a great character for twenty-first-century disciples to relate to. He was out there in the real world, a world with a different set of values and principles. He had to work out what serving God above everything else would look like in his life. I bet you can already see similarities between the challenges you face and the challenges that Daniel and his friends had to overcome.

Sometimes when we enter the world of work, we receive a new rulebook. We speak a different language and are invited into a new way of thinking. We learn about the "corporate culture" of this place of employment—what we're expected to give and what we'll get in exchange. Our name, our very identity is changed. God is no longer our judge, or even our provider. The corporation, our career will protect our life now. If we meet the expectations of the company, no matter what they are, we'll have a steady paycheck, health insurance, money for mortgage and car payments, perhaps even a college fund for the kids. We find worth and value in our professional achievements.

So why not be wined and dined by all this? It can promise us so many wonderful things. We get to enjoy opportunities for personal development and promotions. Our bills are paid and our families are provided for.

But there is no such thing as a free lunch.

Such a choice will cost us a great deal. Many of us have lready paid the price in family time, friendships, health, and marriages.

We may raise our children and unintentionally disciple them in these values. We want them to participate in activity after activity: ballet

> PEOPLE SHOULD
> NOT HAVE TO
> CHOOSE BETWEEN
> SERVING AT
> CHURCH AND
> SPENDING TIME
> WITH THEIR
> FAMILIES.

classes, sports teams, music lessons, clubs, and organizations. These will look great on the résumé in the years to come. Their college applications will have the edge that no one else's has. Maybe they will get chosen. It is a privilege, after all, to be chosen to do so much, to be involved in so many things. Shouldn't we invest in all that potential?

But at what cost? Is there anywhere we will draw the line and say no? Learning to say no in order to protect our need for balance of work and rest is a valuable skill that many of us need to develop and then put into practice. If you say yes to everything that comes along, you're likely saying no to quieter but no less important things such as rest and retreat.

These demanding values have even entered the church. We ask our leaders to be on call 24/7 and are offended if they cannot respond because they are having some time off. One young pastor fresh from seminary interviewed at a church where he was well received. Conversations progressed to extending a call for him to serve as pastor of that congregation. The young man proposed one designated day off each week. The talks fell apart right then. Members of the congregation could not imagine why he would want to draw away from them even for a day. Their needs would not stop for that day. Other pastors begin new positions with as little as one or two weeks of paid vacation each year, just as if they were beginning a new position making burgers and fries. The demands that pastoral work makes on time and energy, the many days of long hours, the price that ministry families often pay, simply do not enter the equation.

We push our church staff to work harder, perform better, and produce more fruit. We want better leaders, we want success. Sacrifice is part of the call.

We leaders can get so concerned about filling empty spots in the volunteer roster that we pressure people to give of their time in a way that is not wise or healthy! People should not have to choose between serving at church and spending time with their families. Life should be in balance.

"BUT YOU HAVE NO IDEA WHAT IT'S LIKE!"

People have said to me, "Mike, I hear what you are saying, but you have no idea what is going on out there. I am part of this corporation and it's crazy. It takes up every part of my life. My family is just an afterthought, tacked on to any spare moments I have."

I say, "Have you thought about getting another job? If you have the opportunity to be a free man, then why be a slave?"

"But you don't understand."

"OK, so why don't you witness then?"

"What do you mean?"

"Tell them the good news. Tell them that you don't have to work all the time and you can produce just as much."

"Yeah, but you don't know my boss...."

You're right. I don't know your boss. I don't know the unique

> AS CHRISTIANS WE'VE GOT TO HAVE FAITH THAT THERE IS ANOTHER WAY; THAT WE CAN OFFER AN ALTERNATIVE WAY TO LIVE, AND IN THAT LIFE WITNESS TO OTHERS.

demands that your family faces. I don't know your church situation. But you know what? I believe as Christians we've got to have faith that there is another way; that we can offer an alternative way to live, and in that life witness to others.

This is so important for today's Christians, especially in the Western world. This is gospel. This is good news. This could literally transform thousands of lives. It could heal thousands of families. It could transform thousands of churches. We would start seeing fruit, because we choose to abide.

Have you tried the Daniel Test?

THE CHOICE

The first decision that Daniel made was internal. For a young man hundreds of miles away from home, the opportunities offered must have been tempting. He had been given a shot at the fast track to status and power.

But he had to work out what his values were, what he stood for before he went any further. His name was Daniel, "God is my judge," not Belteshazzar, "Bel protect my life."

The same is true for us. The first step is an internal decision about what is most important to us. We easily forget that God is our real boss and the real provider of all our needs. We have to choose not to feed ourselves with all the tempting offers that come at such a high price. Sometimes we are motivated to work so hard because we have to pay for things that we could not afford in the first place. We buy into the view that a huge house and new car prove we are successful. One company offering services in debt reduction runs a television commercial about a smiling

> INSTEAD OF CHASING AFTER THE DREAMS AND VALUES OF THE WORLD AROUND US, WE NEED GOD'S PERSPECTIVE.

man who is proud of his large house, expensive car, country club membership, and so on. And how does he do it? By living in debt up to his eyeballs!

We seem to compete with our families, friends, and neighbors. Maybe we even compete over how talented our children are. Johnny is in this program for gifted children, and Susie has been accepted into that exclusive program. For some of us, the issue may even be pride: We like the idea that we can keep on working way beyond the norm and come out looking better than everyone else.

> When I was ten years old, we moved from Nottingham to Durham. In Nottingham I had been swimming with a local club on Saturday mornings. In Durham the only swim club met on Sunday mornings. My parents chose not to send me to the club at a time that clashed with a strong family priority—worship with other believers. I was disappointed, but I look back on it as an important lesson in making value based decisions. Many families make decisions that superficially look positive for their kids but have long term consequences that outweigh the short term advantages. Establishing a rhythm in family life means that we sometimes have to make decisions that go against the grain.
>
> —Mark

We have to choose to put our lives, careers, and families into God's hands again. Instead of chasing after the dreams and values of the world around us, we need God's perspective. Let's prioritize our God given relationships and allow God to vindicate us. Jesus puts it like this:

> But seek first his kingdom and his righteousness, and all these things will be given to you as well.
>
> —Matthew 6:33

Families are too busy doing extracurricular kids' activities. Often the first thing to go is Sunday worship or children's activities at church. In reality, this doesn't create more space; the family just fills the slot with something else. A busy family is not necessarily a happy one.

Joe, our eldest son, joined a soccer club. Before long the club decided to start meeting on Sunday mornings. Sunday morning is the time we worship as a family at church, so we had to find another club. It can be hard to resist cultural pressures and model a rhythm of life that incorporates times for rest, recreation, and God.

It's also hard to resist pressure to join everything that's offered! Our younger son, Daniel, goes to a theater-arts school. He's a great actor and gets promising feedback. Recently the forms came out for kids who wanted to sign with an agency. The glossy brochure looked tempting. What parents wouldn't want their child to do well in something the child enjoys? It was also tempting because Daniel shows great potential! However, we felt that at age six he was too young. It would probably be too much for Daniel. Also, it would put too much pressure on our family rhythm.

—Mark and Penny

Simon and Sue were both schoolteachers. When they had children of their own, Sue gave up work to focus on the children. Simon found that he could easily spend so much time working that their family time suffered. He made the decision to cap the amount of time he

gave to preparation for teaching. He
realized that there would always be
something else to do, but that there
wouldn't always be the opportunity
to invest in their family in such a
significant way.

Simon had to go against the flow in
order to do this.

> ARE THERE AREAS
> IN YOUR LIFE
> WHERE YOU HAVE
> TO GO AGAINST THE
> FLOW IN ORDER
> TO ESTABLISH THE
> RIGHT RHYTHM?

Are there areas in your life where you
have to go against the flow in order to establish the right rhythm?

Daniel asked for permission for himself and his friends to eat
differently for a period of time. If they looked worse at the end of the
test, they would go back to the royal diet. If not, they could continue.

Wouldn't it be something if Christians said to their bosses, "I'd like
to take a day off, a full, proper day, and I'm going to produce more
when I do work. I am going to be more effective in this company.
Jesus says, "Unless you abide, you can't bear fruit." Don't you think
that would be a really helpful witness? Don't you think God would
back you up because he made you that way? Sure, he would.

Employers won't lose out; in fact, they only stand to benefit.

Ros was working through this issue when she worked for a large
corporation in London. The demands of working, commuting, and
running a home single handedly, as well as having significant church
leadership responsibilities, were proving too much.

Ros decided to request to work a four day week, with only slightly
longer hours on these days and a reduction in pay. The company

was happy with the plan. This enabled her to have a regular day for recreation and rest. The weekends weren't full of catching up with household jobs; she could actually have some fun. A new pattern of working from rest was established at this time. It was good news for her employer; Ros was at least as effective as before.

Daniel was healthier for living the way God wanted him to. In addition, he and his friends were more effective and were given positions of influence and opportunity.

And it actually works!

When I led St. Thomas' Church, the staff had six weeks of vacation a year. They were allowed one day of retreat time a month and through the summer vacation (July and August) were allowed to work only half days and spend the rest of their time with their families or with their friends. Our junior staff was given four weeks of vacation a year. Yet the church became one of the fastest growing churches in England at that time, in a city where less than 2 percent of people went to church. Eighty percent of our church was under the age of forty, a generation often missing from today's church. It was God who grew the church, not our striving to make something happen.

Pastors would come to me with bags under their eyes and burdens on their backs. They would ask, "What are you doing that I need to do?" What they were actually asking was, "What's the extra little thing that I need to do, even though I'm absolutely burned out and beat up?"

I'd say, "Play golf. Take a day off with your wife. Enjoy your family." They thought I was just being cute, so I had to keep on saying it until they really believed it. Fortunately, because they wanted the kind of fruitfulness that they saw in my ministry, they did listen from time to time.

Some leaders hearing about the rapid growth at St. Thomas' came to learn the secret of our apparent success. Many of them commented on the amount of rest and prayer that was built into our schedule. One actually said, "I don't know how you can get so much done by doing so little!"

> PEOPLE CAN PRODUCE MORE BY DOING LESS.

You might be surprised to find that, at times, people can produce more by doing less.

When we discover God's rhythm for our lives, work from rest, retreat and adventure, abiding and bearing fruit, we tap into something that God has stored up for us since the first days of creation. We rediscover the kind of workers he made us to be, and we experience the benefits.

> Often we see new clubs or classes open and kids sign up and buy all the equipment. For a while they are really excited. Then the children or their parents get tired of it and they drop out. Their busy lives are already too full; they can't fit another thing in! One of the benefits we see for our own kids is that generally they start a new recreational activity and stick to it. We think this is because we don't take something on unless it fits into the family schedule. In the long term, this saves a lot of wasted time, energy, and money.
>
> —Mark and Penny

Dave and his wife, Janelle, moved from Pittsburgh to join the team at St. Thomas' in Sheffield, England. Janelle started teaching in a local school and Dave became the youth pastor at the church. He had a lot going on. He was the consummate evangelical Christian, striving in everything he did. He strove to make the ministry work, he strove to get leaders, and he strove to get kids to come to church. One day when he walked past my office, I called him in.

"Hey Dave, when did you last take a day off?" I asked. "I spoke to

Janelle this weekend and asked how things were going. She said she hadn't seen you in a long time, and that you hadn't had any time off. So I just wanted to check up on you and see how you are doing."

Dave said, "I haven't had a day off since we moved to England." Clearly he wanted me to know that he had been working hard to get things going.

> IT WOULD BE SO EASY TO KEEP OUR THOUGHTS TO OURSELVES AND CARRY ON. BUT THIS IS NOT REPENTANCE AS JESUS TEACHES.

"Do you like your job, Dave?" I asked.

"Yeah," Dave replied. "I love my job. Why?"

"Well, because you are going to lose it if you don't take a day off."

This completely threw Dave. He was about to lose his job for working too much? This was the last thing he expected me to say.

"So what do you want me to do?" Dave asked.

"I want you to go home, get out a yearly calendar, and put your days off on it. Then I want you to schedule your vacations for the whole year."

Janelle and Dave sat down and scheduled their six weeks of vacation throughout the year. Dave knew that if he didn't put the dates in his schedule then and there, he was never going to take the time off.

Dave scheduled time to go on retreat with me in South Carolina. On the plane journey over, Dave couldn't stop worrying about what would happen to the ministry. When he got home, the team came up and said, "Dave, you won't believe this! While you were gone, seven teens came to Christ and another ten have started coming to the group!"

Dave realized that it didn't all depend on him. There was fruit while he was resting. A few weeks later Janelle and Dave went home for Christmas. When they came back, the news was the same. "Dave, five teens became Christians, and we have thirty kids signed up for our Alpha course!"

By this time, Dave was thinking, *This rest thing is really true. It actually works!*

The next day he walked into my office and said, "Mike, I think you need to give me a sabbatical. This ministry is much more successful when I'm away from this place!"

CAN WE TAKE THE DANIEL TEST?

Twenty-first-century disciples are called to live differently from the world. This is possible, but like Daniel, we may need to take some risks.

Do you choose to challenge the culture you are part of by offering it some good news that it doesn't have to be this way? Good news—you can be more effective in life when you work from rest.

It may be a struggle, and it may mean that you don't take that promotion. It may mean you turn down that particular job. It may be that your lives have to change. Perhaps your family life has to change. And these things are difficult.

> LIFE AS A
> DISCIPLE
> IS OFTEN
> SIMPLE TO
> UNDERSTAND
> BUT HARD TO
> DO.

It may be that you need to address some of the choices you make that are a result of the pressure you are under. Perhaps you have invested too much of your identity in the workplace or your children's achievements. Perhaps you overwork because you think it is spiritual; perhaps it's a pride thing. Or maybe you have to look again at the lifestyle choices you've made, such as big spending, which have produced big debts that require heavy work hours to pay for.

Life as a disciple isn't easy. Sometimes we expect it to be complex, but easy. The truth is that life is often simple to understand, but hard to do.

God's call to us is that we should chew on these issues, work through them, and see what we need to apply to our own situation.

Where could you apply the Daniel Test to your life?

THE CIRCLE IN RHYTHM

> "The time has come," he said. "The kingdom of God is near. Repent and believe the good news!"
>
> —Mark 1:15

As you consider how and where you might need to apply the Daniel Test, it might help to review the Circle. Changing the rhythm of life is often a significant kairos moment. We don't want to make rash decisions that we don't follow through on. Instead we need to take time to go through the process of repentance and belief, to see God's kingdom extended in this area of our lives.

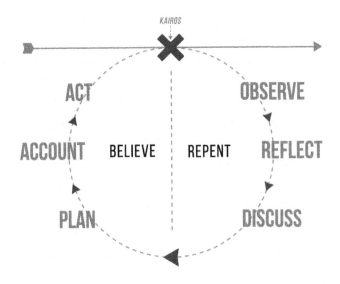

OBSERVE. Spend a week looking at your life. Watch how well your relationships work. Observe your times of rest. Look at your involvement in church activities. Observe your work life. Consider how much time you spend thinking about or talking about work after hours. Observe the pressure points in your day and your week. Watch how you spend your day off. Take note of what is going through your mind during your downtime. Look at what the Bible says about rest.

REFLECT. Ask yourself some questions. *Do my values reflect the world around me, or the way God has created me to live? Why do I find it hard to rest? Are my relationships healthy? Do I work too many hours?* Spend time in prayer and in God's Word. *What does God say about how I am living my life?*

DISCUSS. Daniel didn't go it alone. He had three friends who lived it with him. Talk to your spouse or someone else you love and trust about the challenges you face and the ways you need to change your life.

PLAN. Come up with a plan for change. Do you need to ask for a change in your work hours, or even look for a new job? Do you need to ask for help from within your community of friends so that you can have some time off? This may require some creative thinking. What particular things do you need to ask God to provide so that your life can change? Write it down.

ACCOUNT. Talk with your friends again about the plans you are making, and see if they have any feedback. Get your friends to pray with and for you about the steps you are trying to take. If needed, be accountable about when you are going to start to implement the plan.

ACT. Do it!

As we grow as Christians, we tend to learn a lot of valuable information, much of which remains jumbled and unpacked within the confines of our minds. We know a lot of "stuff" but can never quite figure out how to use it. Learning the Semi-Circle, and indeed all of the LifeShapes, will equip you with the structure and focus you need to take this information and learn how to apply it to your life. The principles of work and rest may have seemed difficult to apply at first but hopefully you are beginning to gain a clear understanding of how you can implement these important changes in your life. Make no mistake, these are important changes to make if you are to lead a life of discipleship. Jesus' teachings and examples of work and rest are no less valuable and vital than any of the other lessons he taught.

CHAPTER 8

THE SABBATH MAKES AN EXODUS

After several attempts, the Israelites left Egypt and were finally
free! In the weeks following their great escape, they saw God do
amazing things.

After letting God's people go, Pharaoh changed his mind and pursued
them with his army, so God opened up the Red Sea for the Israelites
to walk through. As they traveled through the desert on the other
side, God gave them manna and quail to eat. When they needed
water, he made it gush from a rock.

After three months of traveling through the desert, the Israelite
community reached Mount Sinai. Here God set out the boundaries
of the covenant relationship he had with the Israelites by giving them
the Ten Commandments.

God said to his people, "These are the top ten things to do and not to
do."

Included in these laws are commands not to murder, steal, or commit adultery. Thousands of years later, we still take these commandments seriously. Even though we have been saved by grace, we see the benefits of living according to the Ten Commandments. Nobody thinks murder is a great idea, nor stealing, nor committing adultery. But among the Ten Commandments is a certain one that has become too easy to forget.

> Remember the Sabbath day by keeping it holy. Six days you shall labor and do all your work, but the seventh day is a Sabbath to the LORD your God. On it you shall not do any work, neither you, nor your son or daughter, nor your manservant or maidservant, nor your animals, nor the alien within your gates. For in six days the LORD made the heavens and the earth, the sea, and all that is in them, but he rested on the seventh day. Therefore the LORD blessed the Sabbath day and made it holy.
>
> —Exodus 20:8–11

In other words: *Take a day off!*

You need a day off. Both men and women need a day off. Your children need a day off. For those of you in positions of responsibility in the church or the workplace, your staff needs a day off. Every color, class, and culture needs a day off. From the highest in society to the poorest of the poor, the commandment is the same: *Take a day off.*

This is not a mere suggestion. It's a commandment, right up there with the stuff about murder and stealing and adultery. If you don't take a day off, then you have broken God's law. From God's perspective all of the commandments are equal. Murder and not having a day off are on the same level.

It doesn't get easier to understand, which is what God is saying. This is really important because it is fundamental to our design specification; this is a creation ordinance. Men and women need a day off. Yet we never teach it to anybody. We don't live it, we don't disciple anybody in it, and our churches don't reflect it.

> IF YOU DON'T
>
> TAKE A DAY
>
> OFF, THEN
>
> YOU HAVE
>
> BROKEN
>
> GOD'S LAW.

When someone works extra long hours to get a project done, we too often think, "Good job!" But the truth is, hard though it is for all of us to face, when we don't take a day off, we are doing something wrong. God makes it absolutely clear that this is not some kind of negotiated settlement between him and us. This is the order of things.

FLIRTING WITH BURNOUT

Let's pursue a line of thinking for a moment. What are the consequences of not following God's pattern? What are the consequences of not living in rhythm with life?

A friend of mine who teaches LifeShapes has taken the pendulum and further developed the picture of the Semi-Circle because he's been conscious that many of the people he works with are flirting with burnout all the time. His picture looks something like this: You've got rest and you've got work, and then you've got the "burnout danger zone."

Instead of allowing the pendulum to swing naturally back from work to rest so that we abide, we push it a little farther in an unnatural direction. We say, "We'll be all right. We just need to gun it. We just need to press through this busy phase. We're going to be OK. It's going to be all right. We'll take a break later. We'll get a break next

> WE PUSH
> OURSELVES
> UNTIL WE GET
> ILL, AND THEN
> WE'RE RELIEVED
> BECAUSE WE HAVE A
> LEGITIMATE REASON
> TO TAKE TIME OFF.

month. It's going to be fine. We'll just keep going, because if we can keep going then we're going to make those deadlines and ..."

Or we push ourselves until we get ill, and then we're relieved because we have a legitimate reason to take time off. It's as though being sick or put on bed rest by a doctor is more appropriate than rest.

Even reality television shows tell us that this is an acceptable way to live. One of my favorite TV shows is Discovery Channel's *American Chopper*. This father-and-son team builds one-of-a-kind motorbikes while shooting hysterical exchanges back and forth. But what is it with the deadline thing? It's always the same. "We're never going to make it ... we're going to have to stay up all night and all day and all weekend and ..." ABC's *Extreme Makeover: Home Edition* is another one—they tear down a house and rebuild it in seven days, complete with furnishings and custom design. They're always going down to the wire. Thirty minutes before the family is due to come home, the crew is running around hanging pictures and tossing pillows.

Shows like these are a reflection of the pressure we *all* face in our own lives, and which the culture seems to value. We start to believe that this is the American way of life. You've just got to keep pushing through. Go on to the next frontier. OK, try it. You'll soon have the smell of something following you around. The edges of your life will become singed, and before you know it everything will be an inferno. If you keep pushing, you get into the burnout zone. The best that you can hope for is that you collapse into your rest. Instead of the pendulum swinging back gracefully to its point of rest, you've pushed it all the way around and it crashes into rest. The best that you can do is to take some rest as it swings by on its way through to do some more work.

Why do we do this? Well, we probably do it for all kinds of reasons. We feel it's the right way to do things. We believe it's the way to be most productive. We feel that it's the expectation of our culture and community and career. We may even feel that it's the expectation placed on us by those around us, by the people we love.

HALT!

The burnout zone is a dangerous place to live. When we do not take time to rest, we get beyond the point of tiredness. Soon we are simply living off adrenaline.

Adrenaline is deceptive. It can feel great in the moment, but the truth is we are as tired as ever. Eventually we get to a point where even adrenaline won't carry us any longer. We end up making decisions we wouldn't have made if we had given ourselves the time and rest to get some perspective. How many of us have said or done something we regretted because we were caught off guard?

Don, a friend of mine at Indian Hills Baptist Church in Arkansas, shared something helpful. Don used the acronym HALT to describe four places where we are vulnerable to temp tation and are likely to be caught off guard. We could apply this acronym to many circumstances in life. We are particularly exposed in these four areas, one of them being rest, which can then compound the effects of the other three.

We need to be on guard against temptation when we are:

HUNGRY. What do you do when you are hungry? Our appetites cry out for attention. It could be for food. When we are working long hours, we barely get the chance to eat regularly, let alone healthily. But we could be hungry for other things, such as affirmation, sex, or control. These appetites can be kept in check, but when we are doing too much, we don't have time to pay attention to or deal with our appetites. We are so tired that we are not alert to times when we are being drawn into temptation. We are in danger of choosing to satisfy our appetites above everything else that matters to us.

ANGRY. What are you likely to do when you are angry? What are you likely to say? You are overworked and the adrenaline has run out. You get home to find the kids being rambunctious. Normally this is no big deal, but this time it's too much and you completely overreact. Voices raise, doors slam, children cry. Before you know it, you have upset everyone in the house and no one is talking to you. By then, you feel that even your spouse has taken sides against you. And what did you gain? You're still angry.

LONELY. When we push ourselves to work beyond our limits, there is no time to live a balanced life. We have no time to maintain a relationship with God or to spend time with friends. Maybe the demands of the office have kept you away from your normal church routine. Perhaps work has taken you away from home. But just being busy doesn't mean that you don't crave company, that you don't need intimate relationships. Loneliness surfaces when you are far from friends and family. You are so worn out that you are desperate for relationships.

TIRED. You have overworked for months. It has been weeks since your last day off. Even then you took some work home. You feel the pressure both at work and at home. When you arrive home, all you want is some space, a chance to unwind with no expectations.

Tonight you would love to stay home alone and watch a movie, but you've promised the kids you would play softball. It's not the first promise you've made to do so, but every other time something came up. You have no energy or enthusiasm to go out, but your family is getting frustrated with broken promises. And you are tired of their expectations. You provide the money for a good home and food on the table. What more do they want from you? Does no one see what you do for this family?

Take a long look at your life and the times you have burned out, or come close. How do you behave when you are:

Hungry?
Angry?
Lonely?
Tired?

Perhaps only one of the four relates to your situation. Or maybe you see all of them operating in your life right now. If that is the case, you need to do something fast. Sometimes we insist that we cannot afford to take a day off. We say things like, "I don't have time to take time off." "My work is too important." "No one else can do what I do."

When you feel overwhelmed by juggling work, church, relationships, and God as it is, rest seems like the last thing you should do.

But when we think of the potential damage overwork can do to our health and our relationships, can we afford not to rest? In the *The Bourne Supremacy* by

> WHEN WE THINK OF THE POTENTIAL DAMAGE OVERWORK CAN DO TO OUR HEALTH AND OUR RELATIONSHIPS, CAN WE AFFORD NOT TO REST?

Robert Ludlum, the hero, time and time again, recalls some words that have resurfaced after major memory loss: "Rest is a weapon. Don't forget it."[21]

It's easy to forget or devalue how important rest is.

It's also easy to see why God commanded rest. He knows how much we need it to function as healthy and whole people. He also knows that left to our own devices, we'll just keep going.

> In my life I have found rest isn't merely important; it is decisive. When I am rested, I am far more effective at hearing God, responding to his work around me, and in building good relationships inside and outside of the church.
>
> —Mark

HELP!

Sometimes we feel that we simply cannot take a day off. Work is one thing, but how do you take a day off from your children? If they are demanding your time, attention, and energy, then you are working 24/7. Maybe you need to learn to ask for help.

> A number of years ago, we lived in an urban area of London called Brixton. Our children were very young, we had a teenage foster daughter, and some of our staff team lived in our house. There was no such thing as space or "me time." Our extended family lived many miles away; we had little money and no supportive community to speak of. It was a tough and lonely place to be. I began to pray that God would provide me with a friend, someone I could relate to.
>
> A few months later a new Methodist pastor moved into the area. He was married with a young family. They even

---

25. Robert Ludlum, *The Bourne Supremacy,* (New York: Random House, 1986).

owned the same kind of car we had. It wasn't long before David and Jayne became our good friends.

David and Jayne discovered that, like us, they found it hard to have a day off and make time for each other. We came up with a plan. Together we bought a double stroller and a portable crib. David and Jayne took Mondays off. On Mondays I had six children.

But on Fridays, Mike and I had the day off and Jayne would have all the children.

Mike and I spent the first portion of the day apart. I would catch up on chores around the home. Call me strange, but I find cleaning very relaxing. I would have some time and space to do all sorts of things. At the end of the day, the children would come home to a clean house and, more importantly, a sane mother. We would get a babysitter for the evening and have a date night. Having had time individually, Mike and I would already be refreshed by the time we spent the evening together.

> BECAUSE EVERYONE IS SUPPOSED TO HAVE A DAY OFF, THE PEOPLE IN YOUR CHURCH, YOUR SMALL GROUP, AND YOUR CIRCLE OF FRIENDS ARE IN THE SAME POSITION AS YOU.

We could never have done this on our own; we needed to plan our times of rest as a community.

—Sally

REST IN YOUR COMMUNITY

Because everyone is supposed to have a day off, the people in your church, your small group, and your circle of friends are in the same position as you.

Maybe, like Sally, you are praying for someone who is in the same position as you. Is there anyone in your community with whom you can get together to lighten each other's loads?

Helen was a young single woman who worked long hours. She often worked this schedule because she was single and was bored with going home to an empty house! Sometimes she went straight from work to go out with friends. She was always on the move and got very little rest until she became ill and was forced to.

One day she offered to babysit for her friends, Steve and Lisa. Steve and Lisa had three young children and rarely got the chance to have a date night. Helen figured that it didn't matter what house she was alone in.

When she arrived, she discovered that Lisa had cooked an amazing meal for her. The kids were fun—and finally went to sleep! Helen spent the next few hours reading, watching TV, writing emails to friends, doing things that she loved but normally didn't take the time to do.

She woke up the next day totally refreshed. Helen decided to do this again. And again. It wasn't long before this became the pattern for Helen, Steve, and Lisa. Helen began to see the benefits of rest and began to work more consistent hours. Steve and Lisa enjoyed regular times spent together as a couple.

> Adopting a baby with fairly significant medical problems brought a new and sometimes exhausting pattern to our family life. Grace spent her first six months in the hospital, and as a baby and toddler had extra medical needs requiring hospital visits, stays, and a high level of practical care. We cherished a toddler who, though delightful, was very difficult to care for. This was tiring for us and put a strain on our whole family rhythm.
>
> We were grateful to friends and professionals who saw

this and gave us the opportunity to get the rest we needed. We were tempted to use this time to "work," but we tried to take time out. This made us much more effective in our ministry and family life. We saw how establishing a rhythm of life is essential in such circumstances.

We had a very understanding health visitor who helped us to get financial help so that we could take holidays that were more relaxing and restful. Money was given specifically for family recreational activities, meals out, etc. We were also given prepaid preschool enrollment for two sessions a week.

Just having a break from the practical care was great! Sometimes Mark and I just went out for coffee together. It was a very small but much needed way of "resting" at that time. Our church family cooked us meals when Grace was in the hospital so when we were home with the boys we could spend time with them and not have to worry about cooking. This all helped to make sure our rhythm wasn't completely disrupted by the circumstances.

—Mark and Penny

Are these success stories getting you thinking creatively about how you can improve your own situation or step out to assist in the life of someone else? Everyone needs respite, some more than others. Gill is a childcare provider who looks after several children, some with special needs. On top of the usual child care during the day, she cares for children with special needs in the evenings and on weekends so that their parents can take some time out. She has even taken children on vacation with her. This is a very practical way that Gill helps others to have a break when it would otherwise be almost impossible for them.

Don't be afraid to take a leap of faith and perhaps make a huge difference in someone's life. If you feel the gentle urge to inquire if a family needs help, don't ignore it. It may be too hard for them to ask.

SINGLE PARENTING

Churches that work to establish community find creative ways
to support single parents so they too can work from rest. Single
parenting is a challenge, and such parents might have no other
resource apart from their church community.

Debbie is a single person in the church. Jane is a single mom with
two kids. Debbie is an extrovert and enjoys spending time with
people. She often goes out with Jane's family and helps Jane with her children. Jane, though, likes time on her own as well. This is how she relaxes. This is not always easy as a single parent, so Debbie sometimes stays with the kids so Jane can go out on her own. This is a great example of enabling someone else to spend time in recreation and rest in the types of situations that best suit his or her personality.

> IF YOU FEEL THE GENTLE URGE TO INQUIRE IF A FAMILY NEEDS HELP, DON'T IGNORE IT. IT MAY BE TOO HARD FOR THEM TO ASK.

Betty is a single friend of ours. As she tells the story, God
spoke to her and said that her ministry, or "work," was to
support us as a family in a practical way. This was at the same
time we heard the teaching on the Semi-Circle, so we think
that God was up to something.

Over the years she has babysat while Penny and I have
led ministry events together (work). She has babysat for us
when we have gone out as a couple (recreation), and even had
the kids for a night so that we could have twenty-four hours
away on our own (rest). She has been instrumental in helping
us get our rhythm right, and we will always be grateful.

—Mark and Penny

A church in Bristol, England, found itself in the unique position of having a high proportion of single mothers. Each Mother's Day, a team of people cooked a meal for all the mothers in the church. That way the single mothers got to rest and have lunch cooked in just the same way as all the other mothers. It was a great way of experiencing community together.

When we are in a habit of overwork, it can take some time to implement the changes needed to give our lives a new rhythm. Don't be surprised if it is a lot of hard work, but the investment is worth it.

How were we going to do this? A few years ago this was our dilemma. Up until then, Mark's day off had been Friday. The children were at home and we spent time as a family on this day. We went to the park, went swimming, and did all the things parents of small children do. Then our eldest child started school.

So we tried taking Saturdays for our family day. That didn't work. By midafternoon Mark would start to think about everything he needed to do on Sunday. So we tried a new pattern. Mark takes a Friday afternoon and Saturday. He spends Friday morning preparing for Sunday. Mark often takes Grace swimming in the afternoon. This helps him to start winding down too. Friday evening is always time off that Mark and I spend together. Saturdays are then free for us as a family. We do all the normal things families do: watch the boys play soccer, go to the park or for a walk, see a film, and eat out.

We try to keep the rhythm going even if one of us is away. We limit how often we are away together because we feel it's important for our kids to have our family rhythm continue.

—Mark and Penny

A *KAIROS* MOMENT

Sometimes you start out with the best intentions for your family, but through the years those goals can get set aside as life becomes more complicated. Steve and Jess set a high priority on family life. Their son, Kieran, and their extended family received much attention. At work they were fulfilled and enjoyed what they were doing. But when Steve took on more responsibility, their involvement at church began to decrease.

They spent less and less time being with their church family and with God. At the same time, the attention they gave to their marriage also lessened.

One day they suddenly began to see the areas of their lives that were suffering. There was no longer a rhythm of work and rest. They knew they couldn't just hope things would improve. They had to make the change for themselves. But the crucial first step was recognizing this significant kairos moment and then making a decision to act on it. Don't ignore or downplay those potential messages that you sometimes get, or you'll be missing out on valuable lessons.

What is the key to reestablishing lost rhythm and renewing balance in life? Small steps. Steve and Jess couldn't change everything all at once, but they could change something. For Steve and Jess the first step was to renew their relationship with God by spending time actually abiding with him—not just working—on his day, the Sabbath.

Restoration work is often painstaking and slow. Don't rush it, because what you are restoring is precious. Take small steps that help you regain confidence in maintaining a healthy rhythm of life in the long term. The following chapter will explore how you can retreat to the arms of God for renewal, in order to face your daily challenges with optimism once again.

CHAPTER 9

ADVENTURE AND RETREAT

Two mothers sit on a park bench talking to one another. In front of them their children play on the grass. The sun is shining, the breeze is just right. It's a gorgeous day and everyone is enjoying it. The mothers know that it's a safe environment, so they're chatting without watching every move the children make.

Suddenly, one of the children sees a butterfly. Captivated, she smiles and reaches out toward it and then begins to follow it, trying to catch its beauty. As she toddles, she gets farther and farther away from her mom. The butterfly settles on a leaf and the child seizes the chance. But the wings flutter and the butterfly is off again. At that moment the baby realizes that she's miles from mother.

Now in real terms, the toddler's mom is just a few yards away. But to her, something is wrong. It's as though the little girl's tank of courage is empty. She can't see her mommy anywhere. Her bottom lip trembles and she starts to cry. There in the distance, she sees a dim figure that she thinks might be her mommy, and she runs toward her. It is! She holds onto her mom as tightly as she can.

Mom strokes her hand and leans over and gently kisses her. She says, "It's all right. I'm still here."

> CHILDREN NEED A PATTERN OF ADVENTURE AND RETREAT, ACTIVITY AND REST, IN ORDER TO GROW AND DEVELOP INTO SECURE AND BALANCED ADULTS.

The child fills up her little tank of courage just by touching her mother. And guess what? The butterfly flutters past again. The little girl is captivated. She has already forgotten what it was that upset her just a moment ago and begins to follow the butterfly....

We've all seen versions of this story played out between parents and children in the park. Perhaps you've experienced it yourself. I discovered this particular illustration when I came across various studies in Cambridge, England. The studies presented research by educational and behavioral scientists who were studying the behavior of children. Their conclusions stated an undeniable fact about what children require in their development if they are to grow up to enjoy a balanced adult life: Children need a pattern of adventure and retreat, activity and rest, in order to grow and develop into secure and balanced adults.

If children are not allowed to have adventures, but are wrapped up tightly and never allowed to explore the world around them, they will grow up fearful and suspicious of the world. Children learn by reaching out and touching and discovering what happens in response to their actions. If they are restrained from doing this, they will not understand their own world. Because their nurturing environment is overcontrolling, they learn not to trust the world. They become insecure about opportunities in their future, never being sure what might happen. Children must be allowed to adventure.

Likewise, children must also be allowed to retreat; if they don't, there are consequences.

Children who are left unattended even though they are struggling, who are left to make it by themselves because "it will be good for them," may lose trust in authority figures and those who are supposed to care for them. They begin to look for other sources of help and will not develop balanced, wholesome relationships with other people. In one case, a teenage mother chronically neglected to feed her baby. By the time the little girl was a year old, she was rummaging through the kitchen on her own for something to eat. When adopted later, the girl had great difficulty forming a loving bond with parents who truly did care for her, and held on to a habit of hoarding food, even taking it from garbage cans on the street.

> EVERYONE NEEDS TO BE ABLE TO RETREAT AGAIN TO WHAT THEY KNOW IS A SAFE HOME, AND THEN TO ADVENTURE AGAIN FROM THIS PLACE OF REST.

What children need is a constant rhythm, a consistent pattern of retreat and adventure.

Retreat and adventure.

Exploration and return.

All parents know that the only difference between a toddler and a twenty-two-year-old is the length of the pendulum's swing, because the children always come back. They need to reconnect, recreate, and have that tank of courage and affirmation filled up again so that they can go off into the world. Everyone needs to be able to retreat again to what they know is a safe home, and then to adventure again from this place of rest.

TWENTY-FIRST-CENTURY ADVENTURES

We're all intrigued by shiny new gadgets. How cool are those flatscreen LCD televisions? Or a cell phone the size of your palm that lets you surf the Web? Smaller, faster computers with extended battery time. DVD players and luxury sound systems in the car that takes us to work. Can you even imagine life without these things? With the shiny new gadgets in all our lives comes a deceitful trap. We also expect more productivity from ourselves. As I stated in previous chapters, tools and gadgets make work easier and faster and entertainment more engaging and interactive—so we determine to do even more. More work. Even recreation time can wear us out. We come back from the ski weekend too tired to think straight, instead of refreshed. We need a vacation from our vacation.

> MODERN LIFE LACKS THE RHYTHM THAT PRODUCES SECURITY AND DEVELOPS BOLDNESS AND COURAGE.

When we adventure without periods of retreat, our effort becomes striving. This striving violates the proper rhythm of adventure and retreat. Instead of returning home to find rest as part of a pattern of life and health, we give in to the pressure to keep pressing on. Society has become less indulgent toward people and their families. It has begun to push past the natural rhythms with the need and desire for more. More productivity, more work. Modern life lacks the rhythm that produces security and develops boldness and courage.

Striving crushes our rhythm of life. And just like that little girl chasing the butterfly in the park, we don't quite know what has gone wrong; we just know it feels bad. We don't get up on time and we don't go to bed on time. We dodge Sundays and skip our days off. When we have the opportunity to rest, we crash instead and are back at work before we are fully restored. Family time together is violated. On average, the American father talks to his children for *four minutes a day*. There is no time to return to God as a family to pray together and read God's Word.

> AS TWENTY-FIRST-CENTURY DISCIPLES, OUR LIVES SHOULD REFLECT THE PEACE AND REST THAT GOD CALLS US TO WHEN HE CALLS US OUT OF THIS TROUBLED WORLD.

As a result, our security evaporates. We are hungry, angry, lonely, and tired (HALT). So people reach out for comfort in sex, in possessions, in status and power. But none of these things can replace the comforting hand of the Father in the cool of the day.

We are called to live another way. As twenty-first-century disciples, our lives should reflect the peace and rest that God calls us to when he calls us out of this troubled world. He doesn't call us to retreat so much that we leave the world and hide away from it in isolation. We are called to engage with our world, be productive in it, live life to the full. But that is only one end of the pendulum. We still need rest and return.

Children of God need a pattern of adventure and retreat, of activity and rest, if we are to develop and grow in maturity. We need to invest in this rhythmic pattern and understand how important it is. It's the same pattern as that which God gave to Adam and Eve as soon as they were created.

In essence, God said, "You're going to work. You're going to be fruitful. But you're going to begin with rest. You are going to adventure, but we're going to start with retreat. You are going to explore, but we're going to start with the place of return so you know where to come back to."

That is why in Genesis 3 as God walked in the cool of the day, he wondered where his beloved were. Adam and Eve had ventured out and not returned. God knew that something was wrong.

Have you returned from your adventures of ministry in the world? Do you walk with God in the cool of the day, soaking up the refreshment he offers? Do you personally recognize that adventure is part of your life, but retreat is as well?

Do you know that work is your calling, but rest is your starting place? This is why Jesus gave the picture of the vine and its branches in John 15: abiding, growing, bearing fruit, and pruning.

We need to learn to sense of the rhythmic pattern that Jesus calls us to when he says, "Abide in me, and you will bear much fruit. And having borne fruit, you will be pruned so that you abide in me."

GOD SAYS GO

From the very beginning of God's covenant with his people, he has called men and women to adventure. God says to Abraham, "Go to the land I will show you." Yet throughout his life of adventure and exploration, Abraham had places where he camped and worshipped the Lord. The same was true of his descendants Isaac and Jacob, even Jacob's twelve sons.

Moses led the Israelites out of the oppression of Egypt. Now that was an adventure. Yet through the wilderness, there were times when the Israelite people camped in order to rest. Then from that starting place of rest, the Lord called them onward toward the Promised Land. Every man, woman, and child was on the move again, gathering belongings and setting off on the next stage of the adventure.

This is the story of God's people. Embedded deep within the spiritual DNA of the people of faith is a pattern of adventure and rest. We could look at the lives of countless biblical men and women to see this pattern in detail. But for now, let's look more closely at one character: Elijah.

Elijah is a great example of prophetic ministry in the Old Testament, God's chosen mouthpiece during the reign of Ahab, one of the most wicked kings ever to reign in Israel. When Jesus was transfigured, as recorded in Mark 9, two historical figures were revealed with him: Moses the lawgiver and Elijah the prophet. This was to show the astounded disciples with Jesus that he was greater than the Law and the prophets. Elijah represents the prophets and has considerable stature within the Bible. This is how Elijah's ministry began:

> Now Elijah the Tishbite, from Tishbe in Gilead, said to Ahab, "As the LORD, the God of Israel, lives, whom I serve, there will be neither dew nor rain in the next few years except at my word." Then the word of the LORD came to Elijah: "Leave here, turn eastward and hide in the Kerith Ravine, east of the Jordan."
>
> —1 Kings 17:1–3

Imagine that your first prophecy as a new prophet was something so dramatic.

Now, it's a wonderful thing to discover that the birthright of every Christian is to hear the voice of Jesus. Jesus said, "My sheep listen to my voice." Peter, on the day of Pentecost, said, "This prophetic work is so that all people hear the voice of God." Men and women, boys and girls can understand what God is saying to them. But often when we are first learning to listen to God, we can hear really unusual things. We can't work out what it is that God is saying at all. We're thinking, *Is God speaking in a foreign language? What is he trying to say to me?*

Put yourself in Elijah's place. Imagine that your very first word from God is to say to the king that it's going to stop raining for three and a half years, and it won't rain unless you say so. That's fairly significant. You're not starting with the small stuff; you're jumping right into a high profile ministry. You would begin calling the people that run the TV ministries around the world. You'd expect to be invited to all of the major platforms and to speak at the largest conferences.

So the first word that Elijah heard from the Lord was, "It's not going to rain." He told Ahab, the king. We can imagine that having received and delivered the word of God, Elijah was ready for the tough time that was sure to come. Ahab would throw a tantrum, and Elijah would stand firm. "It's not going to rain." What will be the next thing God wants Elijah to say?

Nothing.

The second thing God told Elijah was, "Leave here, turn eastward and hide in the Kerith Ravine...."

Go and hide. That's no way to start a national ministry. This guy's going to be Elijah. He just heard a message from God that is going to affect the entire nation. But the way that he began his ministry was to hide, to retreat, to get fed by ravens.

The pendulum has swung again.

The whole of 1 Kings 17 is the story of Elijah abiding with the Lord. In the hiding and the waiting, in the abiding, God provided for Elijah. He also protected his life and those whom his life touched. We discover later that Ahab was looking for Elijah so that he could kill him, but nobody knew where Elijah was.

> After a long time, in the third year, the word of the LORD came to Elijah: "Go and present yourself to Ahab, and I will send rain on the land."
>
> —1 Kings 18:1

When Elijah once again presented himself to Ahab, he called together the prophets of Baal and the Asherah for a colossal showdown on Mount Carmel. Elijah and the prophets of Baal and Asherah would offer sacrifices to their gods and pray for rain to reveal who was the true God.

The prophets of Baal and Asherah exhausted themselves trying all day to get their gods to send fire on their sacrifice. Hundreds of them huddled and strategized and kept on trying. Maybe if more of them prayed at the same time. Maybe if they prayed louder. They got more and more desperate in their attempts to get their gods to respond, slashing themselves with swords until they were bleeding. Nothing happened.

Then Elijah rebuilt the altar of the Lord. He arranged the wood. He

> WE CHRISTIANS
> OFTEN SEEM TO LIVE
> AT THE EXTREMES
> OF THE RHYTHM OF
> ADVENTURE AND
> RETREAT. WE ARE
> EITHER HIDDEN AWAY
> RETREATING FROM THE
> WORLD, OR WE ARE
> OUT THERE TRYING
> WAY TOO HARD, DOING
> WAY TOO MUCH.

cut the bull into pieces and laid it on the wood. He dug a trench around the sacrifice. Then he got people to pour water in the trench and on the altar—soaking the wood. And then they poured water again, and again. Elijah prayed a simple prayer and the fire of God fell from heaven and consumed the sacrifice—and even the water in the trenches. God vindicated his name and his word, and he vindicated Elijah. Not long after, rain clouds began to gather in the sky.

Elijah launched into the most significant prophetic ministry in the Old Testament with a courageous message for the king, and then he retreated into the rest that

God had planned for him. It wasn't until three years later that God told Elijah to present himself to the king again. Elijah was prepared to *work from rest.*

You'd think it would be the other way around, wouldn't you? But as we track this pattern through Scripture, we see that this is the authentic Word of God to all of the people of God.

WORK AND REST IN THE CHURCH

This rhythm of rest and work is completely contrary to our twenty-first-century adventures, even within the church!

When a new pastor arrives at a church, we want to see what is going to happen as soon as possible. When we launch people into their ministries, our first words to them are not, "Go and have some time off." We give them job specifications of what they need to get done and how many hours to work. Then we tell them how many extra hours we want them to tithe to the church that they won't get paid for but are still expected to give.

We Christians often seem to live at the extremes of the rhythm of adventure and retreat. We are either hidden away retreating from the world, or we are out there trying way too hard, doing way too much. We even think that these extremes are spiritual—God's will for our lives.

The calendar of Israel had a pattern of adventure and retreat. Beyond the rhythm of the Sabbath one day a week, the people observed the yearly cycle of seasons with festivals that drew thousands to Jerusalem. And when the only way to get there was on foot, it took a long time! So the rhythm of life was set by the fact that they needed to go to Jerusalem and return home at certain intervals. These journeys, these retreats, were opportunities to celebrate God's faithfulness and recognize the cycle of life that God gave his people.

But the pendulum would always swing back toward everyday life. We see in the Bible that when God's covenant people spent too much time in rest and did not take on their call to adventure, a generation would grow up not knowing the Lord.

> One of the small groups in our church schedules itself similarly to the major Hebrew festivals, taking up something of the rhythm of Israel's national life. God clearly emphasized a rhythm to the worship of his chosen people. We see Jesus, the apostles, and the early church building on this rhythm.
>
> As a church leader, I can't emphasize enough the importance of establishing and clarifying a rhythm for the church.

We have:

> **a daily rhythm**—corporate prayer at certain times of the day;

> **a weekly rhythm**—courses like Alpha, small group gatherings, Sunday worship;

> **a monthly rhythm**—church leadership meetings, worship and prayer events with local churches;

> **and a yearly rhythm**—seasons or festivals like Harvest, Remembrance, Advent and Christmas, Lent and Easter, and Pentecost.

The seasonal rhythm is most important because it helps define periods of work and periods of rest for us as a church. We are learning to live out this rhythm together as a church family. For instance, in our staff team we have found out the hard way that to schedule a series of meetings just after a period of activity like Christmas is unhelpful for the whole church. Everybody is exhausted.

We also have learned to make regional adjustments to the church year so that we don't end up trying to hold big events when everyone is away on vacation. For instance, in many parts in the county of Yorkshire, a tradition dating back to the Industrial Revolution is still in place. Factories and steel mills shut down for a two week vacation in May. People tend to take this as their key family holiday. It made sense that we used this time to introduce our abiding season.

—Mark

THE POWER OF RETREAT

In December 2004, a devastating tsunami surged through Sri Lanka, Thailand, Indonesia, and other parts of Asia. The world watched home video footage and dramatic photographs of the decimation. Whole communities vanished in a matter of seconds.

In Sri Lanka, television crews caught a group of Christians building a makeshift church. This, for them, was a priority over rebuilding their homes. They said, "We have to meet together on Sundays and then everything else will come together." Do you think we would have been more concerned about building our homes first, before reestablishing our pattern of community life?

Families can retreat together in many ways, spending time together and with God. The rhythm of life in the family as a mini community includes times of rest and retreat, both individually and as a family. Here are a few ideas:

Pray as a family before meals and with children before they go to bed.

Worship together as a family in church. Consider keeping your children with you in the worship service.

Explore finding a worship conference or family camp that can become an annual tradition that the whole family can look forward to.

Create meaningful traditions for occasions throughout the church year, such as Advent and Lent, as well as Christmas and Easter.

Plan times off of work to coincide with times the kids are out of school, such as parent/teacher conference days, teacher work days, and so on.

"I can't have my party on that night. I'll have to have it the next day!" On Thursdays our son Joe, age eight, goes to Stomp, a key event in the children's ministry of St. Thomas' Church. For him this is an important part of his weekly rhythm of spending time with God. Last year his birthday fell on the day of the first Stomp session after the summer break. Joe decided he couldn't have his birthday party on that night. He went bowling with his friends the night after Stomp.

For us as parents, seeing his reaction to the conflict and the way he prioritized everything was great. It was one of those gratifying moments when you see your kids working it all out for themselves.

—Mark and Penny

In different seasons of life I have had to travel as part of my work. When the kids were small, that was a stretch for us. Sally and I tried to organize my schedule in such a way so that my travel would not stress the family. We would look at how long I could be away and how long I couldn't.

We have found it is important to have regular scheduled times of connection and of times to share simple meals together. When the kids where younger and at home they had a "Daddy's breakfast". Now that they are all adults it is still important to gather together as a family with our children, their spouses, and their children.

We've learned that once we get into a rhythm that is consistent with Scripture, we benefit from it. We look for it and hunger for it and we integrate it more and more into our lives.

How can you develop times of retreat with your children?

Parents need retreat times too. When was the last time you got to spend some quality time with your spouse—doing something that the two of you like to do without the kids getting a vote? When was the last time you talked together about something besides work, kids, or household chores? When was the last time you shared with each other what God is saying to you—or even had the quiet space to listen to God together? Does it seem like an impossibility? With busy lives, it's not always easy to find times to pray or take the time to be together.

Perhaps you need to pray for a miracle through God's provision.

How can you develop times of retreat with the significant people in your life? Your spouse? Your family? Your friends? Relationships are certainly more fulfilling than busy days. A moment with a loved one can change your perspective on your whole day. A cup of coffee, a walk around the block, reading a book aloud together, exchanging back rubs, relaxing with favorite music after the kids go to bed—retreat times can be as small as these experiences. Value the everyday opportunities to tune in to each other as much as the planned weekends away.

We both take individual retreat times during the year. Last year, for the first time, we went on retreat together. God's provision for this was amazing! We were washing up after Sunday lunch when a good friend of ours said, "I think you two need to get away. I'll take the kids."

> RELATIONSHIPS ARE CERTAINLY MORE FULFILLING THAN BUSY DAYS.

We thanked her and said that would be great but didn't think a great deal more about it. A couple of days later we were invited on a retreat together. This was the first time we'd had this opportunity. The children were old enough now for us to leave them for a week.

Without the offer from our friend, we wouldn't even have thought about it. She later told us she felt God had told her to make the offer!

However, the trip was abroad and more than we could really afford. Then, amazingly, someone gave us air miles to cover one ticket, so we went! When we arrived at our destination, our luggage was delayed. At the time this was a nuisance; however, we still enjoyed the first couple of days before the retreat and went on to have a wonderful time. We later found out we were entitled to compensation for our delayed luggage. This covered the cost of the other ticket! God knew what we needed and provided for us in every way!

—Mark and Penny

Sometimes we hear God more clearly and enjoy his presence more fully when we share the experience with people close to us. Creating a rhythm for this kind of experience helps ensure you won't overlook the opportunity in exchange for another busy square in the calendar.

Even if it seems impractical—or impossible—look for how God will work in the circumstances of your life.

FAMILY ADVENTURES

Sally and I have countless memories of times we've taken adventures as a family. We built a tree house in the yard. We've gone on great explorations. When we first lived in the United States, we went on vacation to Florida. One night when the children couldn't sleep, we decided to go to the beach. Dressed in our pajamas, we took our flashlights and went searching for crabs. They were everywhere, so the kids were jumping all over the place. It's one of our most vivid memories.

When the kids were older and we were living back in England, we took trips to the United States and sometimes we would arrive at two in the morning. There was no hope of getting any sleep, so it was time for another Breen adventure. This time, instead of the beach, we would often end up in an allnight Walmart. Time to go shopping!

Because I travel a lot with work, the children have had opportunities to go on mission trips with me. They would come along and join in as valued members of the team, serving, praying with people, being part of God's great adventure.

These are just some examples from our own lives. But you can apply the principles to any stage of family life. When did you last take some time to actually retreat? And that doesn't mean just crashing after a burnout, or checking out from your relationship with God and all the other pressures you face.

When did you last take time to retreat and be with God?

And when did you last have an adventure? When was your last exploration, a journey to a new frontier in your life?

When was your last adventure with God?

TO INFINITY AND BEYOND ...

> Therefore go and make disciples of all nations.
>
> —Matthew 28:19

As Jesus ascended to heaven, he commissioned his disciples to get involved in a great adventure. He still does. Our faith is not supposed to be dull and dry; adventure is a part of the job description of every believer.

But like the first disciples who spent three years staying close to the vine, we should begin from a place of retreat. We should begin from a place of abiding and resting. From there we go into a place of work and fruitfulness and activity, a place of adventure.

We are called to a different kind of twenty-first-century adventure— to live in a different way from the world around us.

CHAPTER 10

SEASONS OF LIFE

There is a time for everything,
and a season for every activity under heaven:
a time to be born and a time to die,
a time to plant and a time to uproot,
a time to kill and a time to heal,
a time to tear down and a time to build,
a time to weep and a time to laugh,
a time to mourn and a time to dance,
a time to scatter stones and a time to gather them, a
time to embrace and a time to refrain,
a time to search and a time to give up,
a time to keep and a time to throw away,
a time to tear and a time to mend,
a time to be silent and a time to speak,
a time to love and a time to hate,
a time for war and a time for peace.

—Ecclesiastes 3:1–8

King Solomon had it all: wealth, brilliant intellect, world power, ambition, and international admiration. But he started the book of Ecclesiastes by saying, "Everything is meaningless."

Solomon took some wrong turns in his life, ignoring his own advice about how to live to please God. But toward the end of his life, he came around again. He looked back and saw that the many diversions he had experimented with were utter disasters—meaningless, futile, and pointless. He wrote this book so that other people would not have to learn this lesson the way he did—the hard way.

By chapter 3 of Ecclesiastes, Solomon was ready to start putting things in perspective. Timing is everything. God's timing, that is. In these verses, Solomon recognizes the way life works. You can't do everything all at once; there is a proper season for every activity in life.

Creation tells us the same story. Spring bursts open with optimism and new life, but summer is chasing its heels. Three months later autumn is right on track, and soon winter blusters its way in. But spring bursts once again out of the winter and the rhythm continues. Night and day. Ebb and flow. Rise and set. Seed and harvest.

And what about us? If we look at the landscape of our lives, we see that we have seasons too. Spring and summer, autumn and winter. We experience an ebb and flow in our activities, a night and day in how we live.

In some phases in our lives we are pioneering adventurers, ready to go out and conquer the unknown frontier. In other seasons we are more inclined to retreat and settle in to something more predictable. Some of us are more natural pioneers, while others are settlers. It's easy to think that only one of these (adventure or retreat) is the way to live. But whatever our natural tendencies, God uses both to help us grow and mature as we go through life.

The different seasons of life present two main challenges:

1. Know what season you are in! Learn to identify where your life is and what God is saying to you.
2. Make the most of the season you are in. Sometimes that will be easy, sometimes it will be testing. But we have to commit to and invest in seasons of adventure and seasons of retreat if we want to grow. The Bible tells us, "Whoever sows sparingly will also reap sparingly, and whoever sows generously will also reap generously" (2 Corinthians 9:6).

The following diagram gives a general idea of the kinds of seasons we go through in life. Eras like young adulthood are more on the pioneering end of the spectrum. This is perhaps the most obvious season of venturing forth into unknown territory—other than birth! But other experiences call us to pioneer to some degree. On the other hand, some stages of life are clearly more settled periods. When you're raising a family, for instance, you want things to be stable for the sake of your children. For some people, their older years are more quiet than their younger years were.

What's your season?

By identifying your season of life, you're not boxing yourself in. You can categorize the various seasons of your life in many ways. You may have some unique terminology that is meaningful to you. These just give some general pointers about the seasons we all go through.

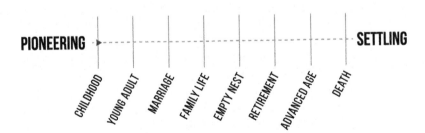

PIONEERING → - SETTLING

CHILDHOOD YOUNG ADULT MARRIAGE FAMILY LIFE EMPTY NEST RETIREMENT ADVANCED AGE DEATH

One of the keys to applying the Semi-Circle is to regularly assess where we are in each season. When we arrived in our present church, we had been married for ten years. In that time we had lived in five different locations, had various jobs, ministered in several different churches, and most recently adopted three children. In each new season we have to reassess whether our rhythm in life is allowing us to have time for rest, work, and time with God. Life changes constantly, so the rhythm needs to adapt accordingly.

—Mark and Penny

Each life change knocks the pendulum in one direction or the other, toward more rest or more work, toward abiding or toward fruitfulness. We need to learn to apply the principle of the Semi-Circle in a fresh way that fits each new circumstance. We certainly don't want to use a life stage as an excuse not to grow or not to bear fruit, but what God asks of us is not the same every moment of our lives. And at every season we need balance, to live in the rhythm of life that God created us for. It's a worthwhile exercise to reflect on what we expect to see in the different seasons of life. While there are some general patterns that come from sharing a culture, individual pictures will be different for each of us.

> WHAT GOD ASKS OF US IS NOT THE SAME EVERY MOMENT OF OUR LIVES.

The apostle John has some words for us:

> I write to you, dear children,
> because your sins have been forgiven on account of his name.
> I write to you, fathers,
> because you have known him who is from the beginning.
> I write to you, young men,
> because you have overcome the evil one.
> I write to you, dear children,
> because you have known the Father.

I write to you, fathers,
because you have known him who is from the beginning.
I write to you, young men,
because you are strong,
and the word of God lives in you,
and you have overcome the evil one.

—1 John 2:12–14

When John writes to a group of Christians, he specifically addresses three distinct generations. To each group he speaks something of God's perspective on that particular season of life. We know that the different seasons of our lives present a variety of challenges. But we can also discover the God given potential of each season as we are living in it.

CHILDHOOD

I write to you, dear children,
because your sins have been forgiven on account of his name.
I write to you, dear children
because you have known the Father.

We already know from the story of the little girl playing with the butterfly (see chapter 9) that children grow into healthy adults as they are given a pattern of adventure and retreat. Whether it's from personal experience or from watching TV shows like ABC's *Supernanny*, we know it's important that all children have a rhythm to their lives. Children with healthy boundaries of love, freedom, and discipline feel secure—and their parents stay sane.

Young children in particular get easily tired and stressed. Sally and I took Beccy with us to Saudi Arabia when she was eighteen months old. The change in the time zone knocked her out of her normal

> AS OUR CHILDREN GREW UP, WE ESTABLISHED BOUNDARIES THAT WOULD HELP THEM DEVELOP A HEALTHY RHYTHM FOR THEIR LIVES.

rhythm. Beccy was beside herself. When we arrived, she wandered around and around in a circle for thirty minutes crying and then collapsed in a heap and fell asleep. As our children grew up, we established boundaries that would help them develop a healthy rhythm for their lives. Our house was quiet after 7:00 p.m. because the children were in bed. We said no to holding particular meetings in our home.

Any visitors staying with us also understood the boundaries. On the other hand, we learned that it was important to stay flexible so that the rhythm does not become a law. We allowed our children "grace gifts" or "grace moments" where they could stay up later because it was Christmas or their birthday. We looked closely at our children's personalities and their position in the family (first born, middle child, etc). Of course, we didn't get it right every time; we've made plenty of mistakes. But doing this helped us interpret situations constructively and made us aware of potential hazards.

Barry and Kate, who had no children, observed the accommodations that some of their friends made for their young children, such as planning outings around nap times or declining a weekend excursion because it would be too difficult to take a child. Barry and Kate loved boating, camping, hunting, sports—they were always on the go. Kate once said that when they had kids, they would just take them everywhere, and the kids would grow up being used to this active lifestyle. They did eventually have children, and quite close together. And guess what? They learned pretty quickly that nap times and schedules are indeed sacred. And while they wanted their children to learn to love the same things their parents did, Barry and Kate realized how critical routine and rhythm were to the well being of their young children.

But *why* is all this so important?

In broad terms, childhood is a season when we are starting out. It's like an abiding time. It's when we introduce our children to our faith. The way we live introduces our children to the love of the heavenly Father, Jesus their Savior, and to the power of the Holy Spirit. The people

> CHILDHOOD IS A SEASON WHEN WE ARE STARTING OUT. IT'S LIKE AN ABIDING TIME. IT'S WHEN WE INTRODUCE OUR CHILDREN TO OUR FAITH.

and the circumstances around us lay the foundations of our adult lives. From them we form our ideas of what love looks like, whether it's presented to us in an accurate way or not. The significant events and relationships of our childhood shape our personalities. They teach us how to eat, walk, and talk.

It's not just through a Sunday school class or vacation Bible school that children pick up ideas about God. It's primarily through their families, and the people around them. Many of our ideas of God have been shaped by our experiences as children. Let me give you a few examples:

- Our fathers were too busy to talk to us, so maybe God won't have the time either.
- Many children of pastors and missionaries never saw their parents because they were busy working for God. They felt that the church was more important than their children were, so it's hard for their children not to feel either resentment or the pain of feeling ignored.
- Though our parents loved us, they often expressed that love when we achieved something. We think, *If I work hard for God,*

maybe he'll love me too.

- Our parents, or even teachers, constantly reminded us of our mistakes, criticizing and never letting things drop. We wonder if God really has forgiven us. We struggle with guilt and condemnation.

On a positive note, some of us were blessed to grow up in families who were able to communicate love, freedom, and discipline in healthy ways that better reflect our relationship with God.

- Families who had time for each other, who enjoyed one another.
- Parents who disciplined, but forgave children when they messed up.
- Parents who talked things through with their children.
- Families where love was expressed not only when you got a good grade or won at sports, but all the time, for no apparent reason.

> ROUTINES ARE NECESSARY FOR SURVIVING AS A FAMILY, BUT TO REALLY LIVE FULLY AS A FAMILY, IT'S *RHYTHM* THAT IS VITAL.

If you grew up in one of these families, you received a glimpse of Eden, like Adam and Eve walking with God in the cool of the day. You saw something of how the love of the Father operates.

What was your family experience like growing up? It could help or hold you back from understanding the Father's love and forgiveness.

This is so important. We need to be thoughtful about each season of our lives. Many of us operate with a survival mentality. We just want this day or this week to be finished. We want that cranky boss out of our hair just for a day; we want the kids asleep so we can go to the bathroom without a little person banging on the door and screeching "Mom!" We sigh more and more heavily as we add things to the calendar, but we keep adding them. If we snap at our loved ones—well, we'll try to do better tomorrow. Maybe the pressure won't be so bad after a night's rest. Then we get up and do it all again the next day without having made any changes that

> THE THREE MAIN BATTTLES CENTER ON MONEY, SEX, AND SIGNIFICANCE (POWER).

would make life easier or family members happier. We don't really think about the overall pattern of our lives and the effect it has. Life is sometimes tough, and you just grit your teeth and do it. We rarely think about fruitfulness, and rest is only an escape from an unhappy existence. Some of us have a routine in place defined by our kids' activities. Routines are necessary for surviving as a family, but to really live fully as a family, it's rhythm that is vital.

> Hear, O Israel: The LORD our God, the LORD is one. Love the LORD your God with all your heart and with all your soul and with all your strength. These commandments that I give you today are to be upon your hearts. Impress them on your children. Talk about them when you sit at home and when you walk along the road, when you lie down and when you get up.
>
> —Deuteronomy 6:4–7

Does my family have a healthy pattern for daily, weekly, monthly, and seasonal life? Or is it merely surviving?

What values are we teaching our children through the way we live?

Do we retreat and adventure as a family?

How are we helping our children to abide in the Father's love in this season? Do we pray with them, read and talk about the Bible with them, disciple them?

YOUNG ADULTHOOD

In New Testament times, people began the journey toward adult life at age thirteen. They were not mature yet; but they would begin to take on more responsibility. They might study, begin a trade, or even get married. When they reached thirty, they were considered fullfledged adults. This is how John addresses them:

> I write to you, young men,
> because you have overcome the evil one.
> I write to you, young men,
> because you are strong,
> and the word of God lives in you,
> and you have overcome the evil one.

This is often a season of struggles and battles that can fundamentally alter a person's life for years to come. The three main battles center on money, sex, and significance (power). They take place during a period that begins during the teen years in the safety and security of our homes, and can continue throughout the twenties as young adults move out on their own.

TEENAGERS

Sometimes we feel that teenagers do not like or want a rhythm to their lives, but that's not true. This is probably the most insecure period in their lives. All teens that Sally and I have come across love to know that certain things are always true and won't change.

> ALL TEENS THAT WE HAVE COME ACROSS LOVE TO KNOW THAT CERTAIN THINGS ARE ALWAYS TRUE AND WON'T CHANGE.

These were some of the patterns we established during our children's teenage years:

- We all eat supper together at 5:30.
- Saturday morning we all do chores together.
- We always have one week of vacation in a beach house at the same time of year.
- Mom always does grocery shopping on Thursdays (a full fridge).
- We have a devotional time at the breakfast table.

These rhythms to family life gave our kids the framework for seeking adventures of their own. Remember the little girl and the butterfly? Well, she's older now and wearing makeup, hanging out with friends (including boys ...), and wants to borrow the car. She has definitely moved on in her adventures. Sometimes we might long for a return to the butterfly days. But she still wants to know that if she looks over her shoulder, her parents will be there.

Our experience has been that teenagers want you there when they return. The adventure may be as small as going to school each morning, to playing sports at night, to big ones like going away to college.

We also encouraged our teenagers in spiritual adventures that helped shape their faith in a way that was not dependent on us. We wanted them to mature in their own relationships with Jesus. When Libby wanted to reach out to the homeless, we got alongside her, encouraged her, and took the food down with her. Her passions became our passions. We got behind her vision.

"I want to be in an A team!" Beccy announced to us one day. "A teams" were the names of small groups for older teenagers at St. Thomas' Church. There were no small groups for younger teenage girls; consequently, a number of them were beginning to leave the church. Beccy had a vision for something we knew needed to happen. So we prayed together and talked through what was needed to get things going. All of Beccy's prayers were answered. She got the smallgroup leaders she prayed for and found new friends in the church. Most importantly, it wasn't our thing. It was part of her adventure with God.

Teenagers need to learn how much sleep they actually need, as opposed to how much is "cool" to have. There is always potential for too much or too little sleep. Neither extreme helps provide a balance for family life. The same is true for eating, working, socializing, spending money, sports, academic studies, and exercising. It's important to regularly assess teenagers' weekly schedules with them so that they learn how to audit this themselves in life as a young adult.

When children reach their teens, they look around for fresh role models. We've often found it helpful to find people who are younger (and cooler) than us and older than our children, then make an effort to include them in our family. We often had young adults from the church come over for meals, or to hang out and watch TV with us. We encouraged our kids to choose an extra godparent during these years, someone that they looked up to who was walking with the Lord.

We need to get alongside teenagers to help them work through their rhythm. If our lives are so full that we can barely hold it together, then how much more important is it to disciple our teens to get this foundation laid in their lives?

When we moved to Arizona, Sam, age fourteen, realized that his commitment to sports was going to be so intense that it could squeeze out his other activities. What about church, friends, family time, and time with our extended family of missionaries here? We live in a place with fantastic weather. What about relaxation by the pool?

As much as he loved sports, Sam knew that he could not commit to it without feeling that his life was out of balance. Sam prayed about it, then talked it over with us and his youth pastor. In the end he chose to get involved in a sport that was less pressured with a short season that would not take up all his time.

Are your teens overstretched?

How can you help them achieve a balance of retreat and adventure?

How can you encourage them in their walk with God?

YOUNG ADULTS

The pendulum swings out even further toward adventure as young people reach the end of their teens and move into their twenties. In very practical ways, there are new things to pioneer. Young adults typically leave home, make new friends, and start their careers. When it comes to a rhythm, whatever was sown in your young children and teens will be reaped when your children become adults. It's important that you are still the coach to the young adult; parenting does not end at eighteen! Twenty-somethings are still trying to figure out how to "do life."

The battles with money, sex, and significance reach a new level as young adults gain increased independence. There are so many big questions to answer:

- What am I living for?
- What do I want out of life?
- Who do I want to spend my life with?
- What do I believe in?

The search for answers can take young adults on all kinds of pioneering adventures. Even as they approach their thirties and forties, Gen X young adults seem to have a thirst for adventure and travel as they seek meaning for their lives. The current crop of young adults (Milennials) is different. Many return to the family home, searching for answers before they step out into adventure. They may

> WE ENCOURAGED
> THEM TO EXPLORE,
> ADVENTURE, AND
> SEARCH, BUT NOT
> AS A WAY TO AVOID
> THEIR STRUGGLES
> OR INDECISION.

try a number of different jobs to find a fit. They also typically have higher levels of college debts to pay. Their adventures start to take shape later on in their twenties.

When I was at St. Thomas' Church, we encouraged young adults to *fully* embrace the season they were in. We encouraged them to explore, adventure, and search, but not as a way to avoid their struggles or indecision. We encouraged them to retreat, but not as a way to hide from life and responsibility.

Both groups of young adults—those who hid behind their adventures and those who hid behind their retreat—had to face the same challenge: This season was where they worked out what they were living for and began to pioneer that path for themselves. These were some of the questions they had to ask themselves:

- How important is being a follower of Jesus in what I am living for?
- Will I attend church occasionally, or get involved and serve in some way?
- What will I give my time, money, and effort to? (This might mean making decisions about the kinds of jobs to pursue.)
- What ambitions do I have? Are they healthy? What are my relationships with the opposite sex like? Are my choices shaped by a fear of being alone, a need to have someone—anyone?
- Do I really believe that God knows my needs and will walk with me through the loneliness?
- Will I commit to the relationships I'm in?
- Will I choose to take responsibility for my own life now?

John describes young adults as strong "overcomers." He also says, "The Word of God lives in you." The struggles and searching of young adulthood make for a season where people can come to grips with their relationship with God. They learn to apply his Word to their own lives in such a way that it shapes their choices about money, sex, and significance. The battle produces victories of maturity that will determine the future. Young adults are at a life stage that has energy and flexibility. There is so much potential!

This season is supposed to bring young adults to the point of being able to establish healthy, independent lives. But it also means a season where the lessons learned from the struggle should produce the maturity to lead others in the future and to create an environment that will provide for and protect others.

For many young adults, this means a new season of getting married and starting a family. Now decisions involve the happiness and wellbeing of other people—and that's a whole new season of life....

CHAPTER 11

GROWING UP AND GROWING ON

A djusting to married life can be quite a transition. You can't just do what you want when you want anymore. Someone else is involved. When you think about your rhythm of life now, you are accountable to someone, or at least you should be. You have to figure out together when and how you will take your days off, how you will spend your spare time, date nights, when and where you will take vacation. It's exciting to share that with someone else, but it can also be challenging when things don't go your way. You've been used to working things out on your own for years; now you have to make it work for both of you.

When we began our married life, we worked opposite shifts! Mark was a social worker and managed a children's home. His day often began in the early afternoon, and he worked through the night. At that time Penny worked in the catering business. Her day began at seven in the morning and finished midafter noon. As you can imagine, we didn't see each other much. This was not an ideal start to married life. If this was going to work, we had to have more time for each other. So Penny changed her job and we worked with this pattern until Mark went to seminary. Then a whole new pattern began. Years later, Penny retrained to work with small children because we realized that Mark's pattern of work in ministry was likely to stay pretty much the same. Penny needed a slightly more flexible job if we were to achieve a good family rhythm.

—Mark and Penny

The transition from singleness to the responsibility of married life and new commitments is often a critical moment, a kairos event. It's often a time when people reassess life goals, look at their history, maybe even review mistakes and past trauma and plan for a different future as a new family emerges.

YOUNG FAMILIES

When Sally and I started out in married life, we didn't think much about living in the inner city, even though we had so much to learn. A few years later when I first held my daughter Rebecca in my arms, something happened. Life had changed forever! I looked at my daughter and thought, *I've got to provide for her. I've got to protect her now.* A new season had begun. We were *parents*. We began to think through things in a different way. We wanted to establish a secure home for our children. That didn't mean we automatically moved out of the inner city.

In fact, we lived in a number of urban areas while our children were young. But our priorities changed. We were used to pioneering; this was a season to settle.

The first few years of married life, while you set up your home and try to get financially secure, are more of a settling season, a time of retreat. The pendulum slows down and moves in the opposite direction. I have seen many young adults struggle with this season. Instead of allowing the settling phase to develop and grow, they look over their shoulders and long for their years of independence and adventure.

Where did the good times go? People feel like they are missing out, or that they "settled" for a less exciting life.

When you are used to adventure and pioneering, the change that comes with giving small children a rhythm can be hard work.

> THE FIRST FEW YEARS OF MARRIED LIFE, WHILE YOU SET UP YOUR HOME AND TRY TO GET FINANCIALLY SECURE, ARE MORE OF A SETTLING SEASON, A TIME OF RETREAT.

Someone once said to me that introverts struggle being parents of children under five, because they feel that they have suffered a takeover of all their space. They never get the chance to be alone. On the other hand, extroverts love it, because they always have company!

When children are small, it can be hard to get a break at all. Disturbed nights, early mornings, constant practical needs can be exhausting. Rest? If only!

We realized at that time in our lives rest meant sitting down for ten minutes with a drink and a paper while a baby was asleep, instead of running around tidying the house. We also had to adapt our recreation. When our kids were babies, we often felt too tired to go out, but we still tried to make the effort. Usually we enjoyed it once we were out.

—Sally

QUIET TIME? *WHAT* QUIET TIME?

We can treat each knock of the pendulum as a kairos experience, a moment of recognizing some truth, and learn from it. Your season has changed; you wouldn't wear your warmest winter coat in the heat of summer. Why try and fit your way of walking with God from a season when you had no children and more free time into this season frenzied with the needs of small children? One new mother, whose son was up at five in the morning every morning and didn't nap dur ing the day, said, "If one more person says I should get up an hour before my household so I can have quiet time, I'm going to scream!"

> MANY EXPERIENCES WILL AFFECT THE RHYTHM OF OUR LIVES, AND THE TEMPTATION IS TO GIVE UP TRYING TO MAINTAIN THE SAME RHYTHM, OR TO TRY TOO HARD.

It's time for a change. Work toward a new way of being with God. Try lots of things; you might find something that works for a while and then you will need to change again. It's OK. There's no guilt or condemnation, just the grace of God.

Patience is the key. Many experiences will affect the rhythm of our lives, and the temptation is to give up trying to maintain the same rhythm, or to try too hard. This is not a time in your life to beat yourself up for falling asleep instead of having a quiet time. Nor is it the time to completely give up on your relationship with God.

The support of the wider community can help a new family. Church members often cook meals for families having a new baby. This very practical act frees up those hectic early weeks with a newborn for the parents to adjust their rhythms in a way that works for them.

How have you handled the change of season? Guilt? Grace? Given up? Use the Learning Circle as a way of working out a new rhythm of retreating with God. Step back from the experience of a change of season and observe the change, reflect on how it has affected your rhythm and talk with someone who knows you well. Then make a plan for a new rhythm of time with God that your friend or spouse can help you be accountable for—and do it.

> It was a cold April day and we were sitting in a freezing cottage in the middle of the Yorkshire moors at six thirty in the morning trying to light a coal fire. The bathroom was in the damp cellar and was so cold you had to leave a sweater on while you took a bath! We had a toddler who was always on the go plus a new baby. The cottage was nothing like the brochure said. And the weather was unseasonably cold, even for England. This was supposed to be our vacation—our rest time. There was definitely something wrong with this picture.
>
> We soon realized this was harder work than being at home, so we went home. After this we changed how we did vacation. We made sure things were as easy and comfortable as possible. While vacations with small children aren't always relaxing, there's no sense in making them any harder than necessary.
>
> —Mark and Penny

One young couple experienced the joy of the arrival of twin boys. They decided for their first Christmas to travel and show off the children to family members in different parts of England. As their vacation drew to an end, they were exhausted and the twins were They came home early. The lesson they learned? Define your limits. We need to learn how to operate within certain boundaries for different seasons of our lives.

COMPARING YOURSELF TO SOMEONE ELSE DOESN'T HELP, ESPECIALLY PEOPLE WITHOUT SMALL CHILDREN. THEY ARE IN A DIFFERENT SEASON THAN YOU.

For many new parents, the adjustment of having young children
is more difficult than they expected. And comparing yourself to
someone else doesn't help, especially people without small children.
They are in a different season than you. grumpy. The time with their
relatives had been good fun, but they had planned to do far more
than they could cope with in that new season as a family.

GREAT EXPECTATIONS

But I thought I would be married by now!
I miss the freedom I used to have.
I love my kids, but I'm so tired.

A generation grew up watching the hit show *Friends*. One episode
features the thirtieth birthday of one of the characters, Rachel. While
her friends try to throw her a nice party, Rachel is in a funk. She doesn't want to accept that she has turned thirty without having done so many things she thought she would have done by that age, including settling down in marriage and family. In this episode Rachel recognizes that the romantic relationship she is in at the time is not going to take her where she wants to go.

> IT IS HARD TO EMBRACE THE SEASON YOU ARE IN IF YOU ALWAYS WANT TO BE IN ANOTHER ONE.

Hopes and longings inside each of us come to the surface at
different times. In the young adult years, unrealized expectations
can be crippling if they are not dealt with. It is hard to embrace the
season you are in if you always want to be in another one. We have
expectations of having a particular career—to be so far up the ladder
at a certain age. We expect to earn a certain income. We expect to

buy a nice sized home. Maybe we expected to settle down sooner. You looked for a life partner, but it just hasn't happened for you.

Whether it is short term or long term, being single presents you with opportunities and flexibility that other seasons just cannot give. But it is important not to get isolated. Without a community it's easy for any of us to go to the extremes of adventure or retreat. Be part of a diverse community with people at different stages of life, have a place to belong, contribute, and be accountable.

If you are not single by choice, it may be particularly tough to make the most of this season. Again it's important to look at the potential of the life stage you're in. What unique opportunities do you have because you are single? How do you take hold of those opportunities in daily life?

When things haven't worked out as we expected, we can head for the extremes of adventure or retreat. We can hide from the hurt by trying to move from one adventure to the next, not stopping long enough to feel the hurt. And at the other extreme we retreat into our own worlds, never stepping out into the risk of adventure.

Are there any expectations you need to let go of so you can make the most of your season?

A MATURE SEASON

I write to you, fathers,
because you have known him who is from the
beginning.

The final group that John addresses is the "fathers." They represent the full-fledged, mature adults, parents in a spiritual sense. They had known "him who is from the beginning," meaning they had an understanding of God that had grown through all the circumstances and the changing seasons of life.

EMPTY NEST

It seems like only yesterday that you were changing diapers and now your kids are gone. They have set out on adventures of their own. After years of retreat and settling to give the children a secure base, the pendulum starts to move again. There is time, space, and opportunity to do something new. By now many people have a level of financial stability that makes it easier to take a few risks. These years often signal a time of renewed pioneering activity—travel, career change, perhaps moving to a new home or another part of the country.

> We have now been empty nesters for a number of years and have had the wonderful delight and pleasure in seeing our children all get married and start lives of their own.
>
> We have had to adjust our patterns of life accordingly. Times of retreat and rest look very different now from the early years when you had to practically schedule bathroom breaks. However we still need daily, weekly and monthly patterns.
>
> Mike and I still eat breakfast together and share the Moravian text with each other daily. We always eat our supper together too. They are the bookends of our day, we may be doing all sorts of other things in between like Phd studying or coaching calls but these times are our connection and reflection points. What are yours?
>
> —Sally

But like the young-adult season, people are often asking searching questions again. What do I want to do with the rest of my life?

Time magazine ran an article looking at how Americans (particularly women) are approaching the different seasons of life.

Now that many Americans, according to a survey, think that full-fledged adulthood begins at twenty-six, there is room for multiple midlife crises. There is the "quarter-life crisis" that hits at twenty-five, the traditional one in your forties, and still another twenty years later. We are living too long and too well to stay settled even in a contented state for more than a few years at a time. And with experience, each new life cycle crisis stands a better chance of looking like just another chance to start all over again.[26]

For many people, that new start can be painful. This later season of life has a divorce rate on the increase. Two-thirds of divorces among people in the United States who are between the ages of forty and seventy are initiated by women. One of the reasons for marital breakdown at this phase may have to do with a newfound desire for a pioneering lifestyle, the chance to do something new after giving so much to raising a family.

This season could be a substantial growth area, if only we would take hold of it. It's a time to reassess, but it's also a time to look and move forward. We need to open our eyes and look around us to see the opportunities before us. Sometimes it means looking "outside the box." It's too easy to get distracted by storing up earthly treasures and paying too much attention to pensions and an inheritance for the kids.

> IT'S TOO EASY TO GET DISTRACTED BY STORING UP EARTHLY TREASURES AND PAYING TOO MUCH ATTENTION TO PENSIONS AND AN INHERITANCE FOR THE KIDS.

26. Nancy Gibbs, "Midlife Crisis? Bring It On!" *Time*, May 16, 2005.

But the questions linger.

What does God want you to do with the rest of your life? How does he want you to spend your time, your money, and your energy?

RETIREMENT

As we mentioned in an earlier chapter, when you look in the Bible there is no such thing as retirement.

> Even when I am old and gray,
> do not forsake me, O God,
> till I declare your power to the next generation,
> your might to all who are to come.

> —Psalm 71:18

We see characters like Deborah, a "mother in Israel." She had her eyes on what God was doing and called others into action. We see men of God like Caleb, who in spite of past disappointments, chose to move forward with God and take his place in the Promised Land.

> IN AN AGE WHERE WE IDOLIZE ALL THINGS YOUTHFUL, THE STRENGTH AND THE POWER OF THE MORE MATURE IS CONSTANTLY UNDERVALUED AND OVERLOOKED.

Other mothers and fathers of faith in the Bible found things more difficult. When God sent the angel Gabriel to Zechariah to announce the birth of John the Baptist,

Zechariah asked for a sign. He was conditioned by the decades of childlessness that he and Elizabeth had experienced.

He didn't want to be disappointed again. This experience had shaped him to such an extent that he was not able to believe an angel sent by God.

How many experiences, good or bad, have come our way and captured us, so that we are locked into society's expectations of us and the season we live in?

In an age where we idolize all things youthful, the strength and the power of the more mature is constantly undervalued and overlooked. Younger generations are denied years of insight and wisdom. The danger is that mature people buy into the values of our times, and only to the rest and retreat part of God's rhythm. Who said that as soon as we hit sixty all we are good for is a few rounds of golf? I love golf, but I am not convinced that it is all God made me for.

Have we Christians locked ourselves in to society's expectations of us? If so, we need God to break the chains of our experience and society's expectations. Then we can take the wisdom of our years and reinvest it in the next generation.

The up-and-coming generation includes your grandchildren, but they are not entirely your responsibility. We are not to run our rhythm around our children's children. Enjoy your recreation, but remember that this is just one side of the pendulum. This is a time for adventure and pioneering, and furthering the kingdom of God—for being released.

Elizabeth's husband was in a nursing home suffering from Alzheimer's disease. Her house was eighty miles from the nursing home, so she opted to rent an apartment close by so she could visit her husband frequently. After he died, she decided to sell her large home and continue to live in the apartment. After all, she was seventy-nine and a widow, and taking care of a house and yard is a lot of work. The apartment just seemed sensible. However, the house did not sell. As the weeks ticked by with the house on the market and few showings, Elizabeth began to wonder if it might be God's will for her to return to live in the house and to help heal a difficult neighborhood relationship. She confessed, "At my age, I haven't thought much about God's will for my life anymore. I figured he just wants me to live a few more years, and then I'm done. So wondering about this is really confusing for me."

God has great stuff for everyone in every season. Don't limit the vision God has for you in this phase of life.

> We have seen rapid growth in the number of young families coming to our church. The church had virtually no kids in it when we arrived. Now we are bursting at the seams.
>
> One of the couples we greatly admire in our church is an older couple who for health reasons took early retirement. However, they still "work." They are a great support to the many young families at church and generally help in many practical areas within the church. They are at Sunday worship every week. They also still find time for their own family, time to rest, and time for vacations.
>
> —Mark and Penny

RE-TIRE?

"When I think of the word retire, I think 're-tire.' God is giving me a new tread for this stage of my journey."

This is how one of the older members of our congregation defined retirement. He and his wife have been active in church life for years while raising their children and being foster parents. With each season they have embraced the call to retreat or to adventure into new things as God has led them. They adopted a baby boy when they were in their sixties. Now in their early seventies, they are raising a teenager. They are still active in church and in their local community. Some of their peers don't quite get what they are doing. "You have worked so hard all your life; you are retiring now. Why take all this on at this point?"

As far as they are concerned, it's just another season living by God's Word, declaring his power to the next generation. Look at your life; understand what season God has you in right now. Take hold of it for all that it is worth. Don't live by society's expectations of your season, but God's expectations, and what you know you are capable of achieving for him. Embrace your season, learn from it, and grow in it!

CONCLUSION

B y now, you've probably got the hint that having a rhythm of life is important. But what is the purpose of retreat? What is the purpose of rest? What is the purpose of this rhythm that produces fruitfulness but begins with abiding? Is there anything else to it?

We'll refer back to Mark's gospel.

THE RETIREMENT MINISTRY OF JESUS

In Mark 8 we come across what Bible commentators used to call the "retirement ministry of Jesus." They weren't talking about the normal retirement ministry that we might think of. Jesus was not leaving employment to work part-time in one of the church's programs, and it had nothing to do with witnessing to the guys on the golf course. It was the time when Jesus was retiring, or pulling away from the crowds. Amazing things began to happen—not amazing things with the crowds, but amazing things with Jesus' chosen disciples.

Jesus is hanging out with the disciples as they travel to Caesarea Philippi. They are still far away from the crowds. The disciples are telling Jesus what the crowds are saying about him.

"Some say that you're John the Baptist."

"I heard someone say that you were Elijah."

"Some people think that you are one of the prophets risen

from the dead."

"But what about you?" Jesus asks. "Who do you say I am?" Peter sees exactly who Jesus is and speaks up. "You are the

Christ" (see Matt. 16:13–16). What an amazing revelation for this disciple!

Both Mark and Luke tell another story of what happened when Jesus was in a time of retreat with his disciples.

> After six days Jesus took Peter, James and John with him and led them up a high mountain, where they were all alone. There he was transfigured before them. His clothes became dazzling white, whiter than anyone in the world could bleach them. And there appeared before them Elijah and Moses, who were talking with Jesus.
>
> —Mark 9:2–4

The disciples are totally blown away! And if that isn't enough, God speaks!

> Then a cloud appeared and enveloped them, and a voice came from the cloud: "This is my Son, whom I love. Listen to him!"
>
> —Mark 9:7

Years later, in his letter to Christians in Asia Minor, Peter talks about the incredible revelation that he, James, and John received that day on the mountain.

> We did not follow cleverly invented stories when we told you about the power and coming of our Lord Jesus Christ, but we were eye witnesses of his majesty. For he received honor and glory from God the Father when the voice came to him from the Majestic Glory, saying, "This is my Son, whom I love; with him I am well pleased." We ourselves heard this voice that came from heaven when we were with him on the sacred mountain.
>
> —2 Peter 1:16–18

Would the confession at Caesarea Philippi have taken place without retreat? Would the Transfiguration have taken place among the crowds?

The answer is no.

Mark underscores this in Mark 9:30–31: "They left that place [the bottom of the Mount of Transfiguration] and passed through Galilee. Jesus did not want anyone to know where they were, because he was teaching his disciples."

Do you see what you're missing by not living in the rhythm of life? You're missing all the best parts. You're missing all the empowering parts. You're missing the revelation that empowers fruitfulness. See, that's what happens in the time of rest.

Jesus basically says, "Abide in me, and let my Word abide in you. Abide in my love, so that you know how to do the very thing that I'm calling you to do as disciples. And love one another" (John 15:9–12).

ANN'S STORY

I worked in the head office for a large English retail company. It had branches worldwide, so I had the opportunity to go all over the world in my position. It was a great job, but incredibly demanding.

I felt that God was calling me into full-time ministry. I'm the type of person who gets a call and follows it, but doesn't really think through what it would actually mean for my life. I took three months off between finishing work and starting at seminary and played golf all summer. It was a great time. But I didn't take any time out to be with God in any way at all.

I arrived at seminary during the weekend of the Ryder Cup. More golf! The competition was in Spain, so I listened to the coverage all afternoon until it was time for our first chapel service. As the chapel service began, I suddenly burst into tears!

I cried for about a year.

Everything that I had placed my identity in—my career, my church involvement, my home, and my friendships—had stopped and had been taken away. My whole life had been based on doing things.

Suddenly I was a student again and was left asking myself the question, "Who am I?"

At the end of the academic year seminary students were sent out to churches around the country on placement for a month. I ended up at St. Thomas' Church in Sheffield.

I was nervous. I was sure that God had been trying to teach me all year to *be*, not just to *do*. But now I was on the job in a church. I wasn't sure what was expected of me, but I had every reason to suppose it would involve a lot of activity!

I met with Mike to discuss my placement. I said rather sheepishly, "I think that God is mainly teaching me about being at the moment."

His response was both a surprise and a relief. He said, "Well, that's great. You are arriving at the time when the church is going into its abiding season. It's when we just hang out together."

So far, so good. He didn't think I was weird. I probed a little more. "So what do you want me to do while I am with you?"

"Just come and play golf, come and hang out. Don't preach or organize any programs. Just come and hang out with us."

Just come and hang out? *Play golf?* Now *this* was going to be interesting. I began to wonder what kind of report I would write about my experience at St. Thomas', and whether anyone would believe me.

On my first Sunday at St. Thomas' Church, I went to all four services. I wasn't looking forward to it. All day long? But when the worship time began with the song, "Better is One Day," I took the hint. The

> MY LIFE HAD ALWAYS BEEN ABOUT ADVENTURE, ACTIVITY, AND ACHIEVEMENT. I HADN'T HAD ANY OF THE REFRESHMENT, RELAXATION, AND RETREAT.

lyrics read, "Better is one day in your courts than a thousand elsewhere."

On that day Mike spoke from John 15 about abiding. He taught that within the context of a day, a week, a month, and a year, we need to have "valley time"—time where we withdraw, retreat into God, into Jesus—before we try and scale the next mountain of adventure, activity, and achievement.

Then he said, "The thing is, if you do not have that built into your life you will try and jump from mountaintop to mountaintop. But if you keep doing that, eventually you will hit a very, very deep valley. And the reason why that valley experience will be so deep is because you have not had the time to process things in the smaller valleys of life."

I sat there and realized that my first year at seminary was like that. I had hit the deepest valley of my life. It was the deepest pit I'd ever known, because my life had been about jumping from mountaintop to mountaintop. My life had always been about adventure, activity, and achievement. I hadn't had any of the refreshment, relaxation, and retreat. I certainly hadn't had that at the start of any work that I was involved in. I realized that God really wanted me to get this message, because I was going to hear it four times that day. At the third service, I went forward to receive prayer, just to begin to respond in some way to what God was doing.

After my time at seminary I joined the staff team at St. Thomas' Church. It was a chance to put into practice the things that I had learned during my placement there. It took me two years to learn what it meant to abide. I didn't know what to do in July and August.

I kept on thinking, *What should I do? I need to start something; I need to organize a program.* I had to accept that all of the programs had stopped, to give me some time to get refreshed with God.

It required discipline to learn how to rest and be refreshed, on my own with God and with other people. It was a discipline to learn how to do some reading, have some fun.

SURRENDER

So we return to John's gospel as Jesus walks with his disciples toward Gethsemane.

"Come on, guys, let's get out of here. Come and abide in my love, come and abide in my Word" (John 15:9–10). The disciples don't know it yet, but it is going to be a long and painful night. In that place of retreat Jesus gives the disciples revelation: insights of the years to come, the tests that would come their way, the help that God would send in the form of the Holy Spirit. Jesus is preparing them for growth and fruitfulness.

For Jesus, the place of retreat was the place of surrender. There in Gethsemane he surrendered to the call that would change the world forever and secure our freedom.

Do you want revelation from Jesus for your workplace, your church, your marriage, your family, your future? Then take the time to abide. Give

> DON'T BE SURPRISED IF THE TIME OF ABIDING IS SOMETIMES PAINFUL. THE RHYTHM OF LIFE CAN MAKE US MORE AWARE OF THE VALLEY TIMES IN OUR LIVES.

yourself the opportunity to hear his word, to abide in his love.

Don't be surprised if the time of abiding is sometimes painful. The rhythm of life can make us more aware of the valley times in our lives. Our lives are so full that sometimes only when we stop do we discover how we *really* feel, what we actually think. As we see in the life of Jesus, times of retreat can be lonely, challenging, and testing. But in that place of intimacy with God, retreat is an opportunity to surrender to him all over again everything that comes to the surface. Our lives can be transformed when they are in his hands.

At the other end of the Semi-Circle, we are called and appointed to bear fruit. We can be productive and bear fruit in the workplace and in our families by multiplying the life and love of Jesus in the lives of others. This is what we were designed to do.

The pattern is simple. It's underlined by Jesus in the final picture and parable that he shares with his disciples. "I am the vine; you are the branches. If a man abides in me and I in him, he will bear much fruit; apart from me you can do nothing" (John 15:5). Jesus wants us to get into this pattern so we can bear much fruit.

God gives us this pattern, this rhythm of life, very clearly. He designed us to work, but we're designed to work from a place of rest. He convicts our hearts to reconstruct our weeks, our months, our seasons, and our years. We find in Jesus everything that we need to build rest into our lives. Only then will we see amazing fruitfulness in our homes and churches flowing out of this abiding.

EPILOGUE

"You've done it."

I had been working at St. Thomas' Church for ten years. In a city where less than 2 percent of the population attended church, the Lord had done great things. We had a congregation of about two thousand people, 80 percent of whom were between the ages of eighteen and thirty-five. My kids were doing great at school and in life, and Sally was happy. My life was fruitful in every way.

Then God asked me to give up leading St. Thomas' Church.

He told me that the job was done, and that I needed to give the church over to the team that I had trained. I had met most of the team while they were in college in Sheffield, or starting out in their careers. Over the last ten years, so much had happened. I'd been involved in their weddings and baptized some of their children. I had watched them develop and grow as leaders and as men and women.

> THE CALL THAT JESUS GAVE HIS DISCIPLES WAS NOT ABOUT FINDING WAYS TO USE YOUR GIFTS OR DISCOVER WHO YOU WERE. IT WAS A CALL TO SELF-SACRIFICE.

We'd laughed and cried together. But now it was time to move on.

I asked the Lord, "How do I tell the team? How are they going to take it?"

He didn't reply.

"Lord, what will I do next? Where do you want me to go?" There was no answer, but I knew in the silence what God was saying. I had been fruitful. The next step, as always, was to submit to the pruning, before I heard the plan for my future.

Surrendering the leadership of St. Thomas' must have been to some small degree how it felt for Jesus to go to the cross. It wasn't because I didn't trust my team; they were and are fantastic. Paul Maconochie, my successor, is an excellent leader. St. Thomas' is a great church. God had done great things. It had been fruitful locally, nationally, even across Europe. Who in their right mind would give that up? Especially since I didn't even know what the next step was going to be?

I was reminded of the call Jesus gave to his disciples.

> If anyone would come after me, he must deny himself and take up his cross and follow me. For whoever wants to save his life will lose it, but whoever loses his life for me and for the gospel will save it. What good is it for a man to gain the whole world, yet forfeit his soul?
>
> —Mark 8:34–36

The call that Jesus gave his disciples, then and now, was not about self-fulfillment. It was not about finding ways to use your gifts or discover who you were. It was a call to self-sacrifice.

In self-sacrifice we find new life. When we give up our lives, we find them.

I knew what I had to do. It was time to surrender to the pruning. And like so many times before, the fruit that comes after the pruning is always more than expected.

"Now to him who is able to do immeasurably more than all we ask or imagine, according to his power that is at work within us" (Eph. 3:20).

After the surrender, God called us to the States. It was then that he gave us amazing opportunities, which included producing the book that you now have in front of you. Hopes and dreams that I could barely imagine ever taking place have occurred because God always keeps his promise. When we learn to surrender to the pruning, fruit always follows. Much fruit— fruit that lasts.

CPSIA information can be obtained
at www.ICGtesting.com
Printed in the USA
BVOW10s0206090217
475638BV00009B/394/P